The Question Is the Answer

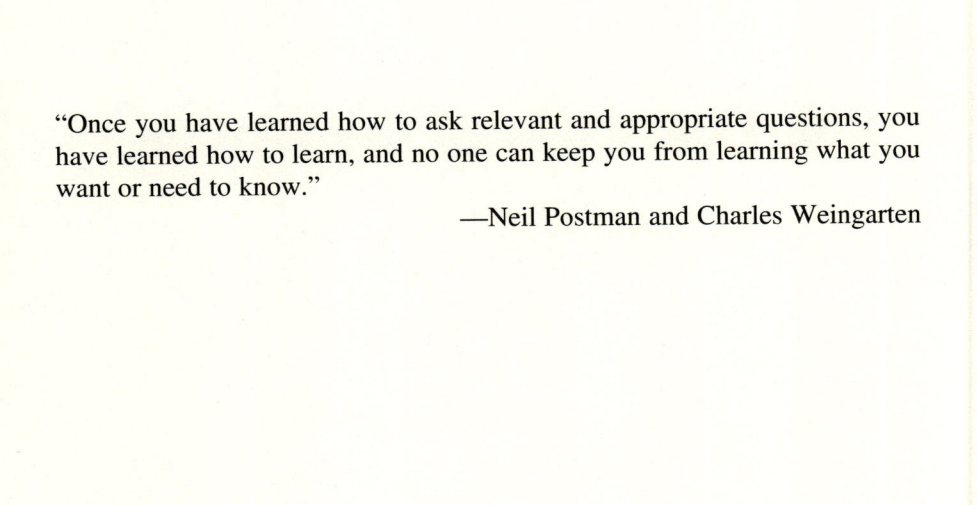

"Once you have learned how to ask relevant and appropriate questions, you have learned how to learn, and no one can keep you from learning what you want or need to know."

—Neil Postman and Charles Weingarten

The Question Is the Answer

Supporting Student-Generated Queries in Elementary Classrooms

Molly K. Ness

ROWMAN & LITTLEFIELD
Lanham • Boulder • New York • London

Published by Rowman & Littlefield
A wholly owned subsidiary of The Rowman & Littlefield Publishing Group, Inc.
4501 Forbes Boulevard, Suite 200, Lanham, Maryland 20706
www.rowman.com

Unit A, Whitacre Mews, 26-34 Stannary Street, London SE11 4AB

Copyright © 2015 by Rowman & Littlefield

All rights reserved. No part of this book may be reproduced in any form or by any electronic or mechanical means, including information storage and retrieval systems, without written permission from the publisher, except by a reviewer who may quote passages in a review.

British Library Cataloguing in Publication Information Available

Library of Congress Cataloging-in-Publication Data
Names: Ness, Molly.
Title: The question is the answer : supporting student-generated queries in elementary classrooms / Molly Ness.
Description: Lanham, Maryland : Rowman & Littlefield, 2015. | Includes bibliographical references.
Identifiers: LCCN 2015026435| ISBN 9781475816884 (cloth : alk. paper) | ISBN 9781475816891 (pbk. : alk. paper) | ISBN 9781475816907 (electronic)
Subjects: LCSH: Questioning. | Reading (Elementary) | Critical thinking—Study and teaching (Elementary)
Classification: LCC LB1027.44 .N47 2015 | DDC 371.3—dc23 LC record available at http://lccn.loc.gov/2015026435

∞™ The paper used in this publication meets the minimum requirements of American National Standard for Information Sciences—Permanence of Paper for Printed Library Materials, ANSI/NISO Z39.48-1992.

Printed in the United States of America

Contents

Preface		vii
Acknowledgments		xiii
Introduction		1
1	Inside Inquiry-Based Classrooms: The Research Basis for Question Generation	9
2	Tried-But-True Questioning Strategies	19
3	Questioning Inside Kindergarten Classrooms	33
4	Questioning Inside First-Grade Classrooms	51
5	Questioning Inside Second-Grade Classrooms	65
6	Questioning Inside Third-Grade Classrooms	79
7	Questioning Inside Fourth-Grade Classrooms	91
8	Questioning Inside Fifth-Grade Classrooms	103
Afterword		115
References		119
About the Author		127

Preface

> Asking questions is what brains were born to do, at least when we were young children. For young children, quite literally, seeking explanations is as deeply rooted a drive as seeking food or water.
>
> —Alison Gopnik

It is 6:38 in the morning, and I am busy juggling the two primary responsibilities in my life: first, the mother of an inquisitive five-year old, and second, a professor at an urban graduate school of education. As I bustle around trying to gather my work effects, my daughter begins the day with her rapid-fire questioning.

"Mama, why is the sun behind the clouds? Why do dogs bark? Why did the mirror get foggy? Where do squirrels sleep? How does the car go?" Some of her questions are easily answered, like "Who is gonna pick me up from school?" Others leave me searching both for a satisfactory answer, and for their source. Not only do I not know the answer for "Why does the moon follow me?" but I also don't know exactly what prompted her to think of this question.

Fortunately for her, today I have woken up with an extra dose of parenting patience, so I am happy to indulge her questioning. Other times, I may not be so generous. I am not alone; Willingham (2015) noted that "even the most responsive parents don't answer something like 25 percent of the time" (p. 45). When I've answered what surely must be the millionth question of the morning, I begin to see the overlap between my career as a teacher educator, my former years as a classroom teacher, and my current role as a mother; these overlapping roles lead me to formulate my own questions.

As parents, we know that the "why" phase is a normal developmental phase for preschoolers. We know that these questions are the signs of our children being naturally curious about the world around them. As children perseverate with the seemingly endless "whys," we understand their efforts to make sense of their world. Though our patience may be stretched with the sheer number of questions, we delight in the questions that children ask, and we actively engage them in searching out the answers. We check out books at the library to answer their question, "Can hippopotamuses swim?" We take them to the children's museum when they pose questions about the mechanics of train engines. We guide their Google searches when they want to understand why baby kangaroos live in their mother's pouch. I use the power of social media to check in with friends who are the parents of young children. I challenge them to share their favorite questions they've been asked, and the results can be found in table 1.

HOW TO USE THIS BOOK

I wrote this book for teachers who spend their personal or professional lives surrounded by young children, in preschool through grades six. As my professional responsibilities bring me into the lives and classrooms of elementary school teachers, my primary audience comprises teachers of young children. *The Question Is the Answer* is a teacher's guide to helping young readers generate text-based questions. This book will appeal to teachers who seek innovative, research-based ideas to teach students the "hows" and "whys" of question generation.

I also wrote this book for parents and caregivers, who spend their days and nights answering children's questions with patience. Parents of the 1.5 million children who are home-schooled are a clear audience. Parents will find that this book was written with a practitioner's approach; research and theory are explained in an easily accessible and readable manner. I strive to provide practical suggestions and easy-to-implement strategies.

My purpose in writing this book is to inspire teachers and parents to tap into their children's curiosity. I aim to help teachers and parents value and promote student-generated questions as a meaningful text-based comprehension activity.

The book showcases how student-generated questions build reading comprehension, promote text engagement, and motivate young readers. I begin the book by exploring what is meant by student-generated questions and reviewing the strong research basis supporting question generation. The remainder of the book showcases classroom examples and scenarios where students are in the driver's seat of generating questions.

The objectives of this book are as follows:

1. To explore what is meant by student-generated questions
2. To highlight the research base for question generation

3. To showcase several familiar question generation strategies/activities
4. To provide classroom examples/scenarios of teachers encouraging question generation with young readers
5. To assist teachers in encouraging young readers in generating questions

Of particular interest to readers will be an exploration of how question generation aligns with the Common Core State Standards. Finally, the book will encourage teachers and parents to implement these strategies in a practical manner with teaching tips, instructional ideas, and other resources.

THE STRUCTURE OF THE BOOK

This book begins with the foundations of theory and research in the field of question generation. This context showcases how the instructional practices discussed in later chapters build upon research and theory on learning, development, and knowledge acquisition. Other portions of the book explore the role and classification of questions in the Common Core State Standards. The main body of the book explores different approaches to question generation in today's classrooms. Each chapter focuses on a different grade level, with examples and graphics to guide the reader in understanding the context. Though I present certain question generation strategies in specific grade levels, almost all of the strategies can be applied to a variety of contexts and grade levels. Readers should see these grade levels as a mere structure to organize the book, rather than a strict guideline mandating which strategy to employ at which grade level. For example, I present "Probable Passage" in the first-grade chapter, but an innovative teacher could certainly apply this to a fourth-grade classroom. I encourage teachers to collaborate with their colleagues to have conversations about how to use a specific strategy in an alternate grade level.

Each chapter begins with a quick overview of the relevant grade level so that readers can understand children's developmental context. In addition, the chapter commences with a brief overview of the associate Common Core State Standards. I provide this information in order to familiarize the readers with where children should be in English Language Arts reading skills at each grade level.

The student samples taken from classrooms and homes where I led or witnessed an instance of question generation are one of the unique features of this book. The purpose of these vignettes is to give life to the book. I aim to give parents and teachers concrete ideas to bring life back to the questions that fill the minds of our children.

Each chapter also includes a "Think About It" prompt. These "Think About Its" are complex questions or queries that guide readers to connect the central ideas of each chapter to their own instruction. I encourage readers to secure

Table 1 Questions Asked by Young Children Shared on Social Media

Age of Child	Questions Posed
2	• Where does water come from? • Who was the first person born? • Where does the hole in the toilet go?
3	• Why do chickens lay eggs? • How did the nest get in the tree? • Where do fish go when there is lightning? • What's Grandma doing in the sky? • Why does soap make bubbles? • Why is there blood in my foot? My whole body? • Luca's mom has a baby in her belly. Why did she eat it? • Who put the boogies in my nose? • Why are zebras black and white? • Why can't we fly? If birds can, why can't we? • Why do spiders have more legs than I do?
4	• How do babies learn to talk? • Are all bugs friends? • Can the sky fall on us? • Who made God if God made everything? • If Jesus was born on Christmas as a baby, how was he grown up already to die at Easter? • Why do people get married? • Can we live under the water like Sponge Bob? • Why are there a lot of letters in the alphabet? • Doesn't everyone celebrate Easter?
5	• Why do our hands get wrinkled after we take a bath? • Why can't penguins fly? • Why don't snakes have feet? • What are our belly buttons for? • Why do we drink milk from cows? • How exactly does electricity work? • How did Hannah come out of Mommy's belly? Where does she come out? • Where does the stuff go when you flush the toilet? • How does Santa come down our chimney if the space is too small for him to fit through? • How does hair grow? • Why are carrots orange and cucumbers green? • Do fish ever sleep? • Why did God have to make bees? • Can plants feel if someone or something is touching them? • Why do people get sick? • Why do moms and dads sleep in the same bed? • What does the tooth fairy do with all the teeth? • Why does my hair grow? • What was the first color that our eyes were able to see? • Why do I have two eyes if I only see one thing? • Why aren't there any more dinosaurs?

Age of Child	Questions Posed
6	• Why are apples different colors? • How are we blood-related to our dads if our mommies made us? • How do seeing-eye dogs know how to get places if they've never been there before? What if the person has never been there either? • Why did veterans go to war if they knew they could die? • Are ghosts real? • How do old people get into nursing homes? • How do people become homeless? • Why do I remember my dreams sometimes and not other times? • Do bears and mice usually get along? • Why is sugar bad for me? • Can dogs eat chocolate? • Why are clouds white and sometimes gray? • Can we live on another planet since Earth is a planet? • Where do aliens come from and are they real?
7	• Where do the hen's eggs fall from? • Why is there a crack in the Liberty Bell? • Does cancer make you bald? Do all people who are bald have cancer? • Why is George Washington the only one wearing an outfit on Mount Rushmore? • Why are daddies usually taller than mommies? • How can we save the penguins from being hurt by the oil from the oil spills? • Can ants swim? • Why do some eight-year-olds suck their thumbs? • Why do I need to go to school? • What's higher, the bottom of the ocean or the top of a mountain? • What is a silo for? • Why are pennies a different color than the rest of the coins? • What causes an appendix to burst? • Why do we put "dear" at the start of a letter? • How do earthworms see? • Why are the top and bottom of a map of the earth white? • Why do yellow and red mix to create orange? • Why do men have an apple stuck in their necks?
8	• Why does the clock only go up twelve hours? • How do glasses work? How do I see well with them on? • How do they get soda and seltzer to have bubbles? • Where does the garbage go? • Do dragons exist?
9	• Why does it get colder in the winter? • Why do we let some animals be our pets? • Who invented money? • Do cows eat steak? • Why is it called a chili pepper if it's hot?

(Continued)

Table 1 Questions Asked by Young Children Shared on Social Media (*Continued*)

Age of Child	Questions Posed
9 (cont.)	• Why are fish different colors?
	• Why do girls wear makeup? Who is God?
	• Why do horses sleep standing up?
10	• Where do tarantulas live?
	• How do fish sleep?
	• What does radioactivity do?
	• What is a menstrual cycle?
	• Do girls grow armpit hair?
	• When are people supposed to get a boyfriend?

a blank notebook or start a new computer file that will afford them the space and time to write meaningful reflections in response to these questions. Some prompts ask the readers to generate lists; others ask the readers to make notes about their instructional process. In any case, readers will most benefit from the "Think About It" when the written reflection is done with careful observation and genuine thought. The "Think About It" also provides a fruitful place for teachers engaged in book clubs and students reading this text as an assigned class reader to begin conversations. Those conversations will be the richest, however, when every reader has had prior time and space to write independent reflections prior to group conversations.

This book provides teachers and parents with innovative, practical, and engaging ways to help young children generate questions about the texts they read, the world around them, and the information they encounter on a daily basis. I strongly believe that posing thoughtful questions is an invaluable skill in both learning and life.

As a parent and as a teacher, I have seen firsthand the richness of the questions that children generate. Why, then, do children not ask them in today's classrooms? What about the nature of instruction might discourage question generation? How can teachers effectively guide students to pose questions? What happens in classrooms where kids are asking questions? How can teachers and parents carve more space to honor and promote the delightful questions our children are naturally asking?

This book values the notion that the question often has more power than the answer. In perusing this book, I encourage the reader to embrace not only the questions that children ask but also the questions that we—proficient adult readers, writers, and thinkers—generate on a daily basis. Warren Berger (2014) called this "chasing beautiful questions" and wrote, "What if you found that creative genius does not lie in knowing all of the answers?"

Acknowledgments

Thank you to Tom Koerner, who planted the seed for this book. I am profoundly grateful to my mother and father, who helped me to sail my ship in the stormiest of times. I am appreciative of my current and former Fordham students and colleagues—particularly Douglas Distefano, Jeannie Humphries, Gary Wellbrock, and Mary Beth Kenny. Much love and gratitude go to Cairstin Mills, the RPNS community, my UVA professors and friends, and the Sole Ryeders, who got me up and out. Mike Reist has been my biggest cheerleader. I dedicate this book to Callie—with a kiss, hug, and nose rub.

Introduction

> The best scientists and explorers have the attributes of kids! They ask questions and have a sense of wonder. They have curiosity. "Who, what, where, why, when, and how!" They never stop asking questions, and I never stop asking questions, just like a five-year old.
>
> —Sylvia Earle

The overarching purpose of this book is to explore how to support and encourage young children in generating their own questions. Throughout the book, this strategy will be referred to in two interchangeable terms: (a) *student-generated questions* and (b) *question generation*.

The most commonly accepted definition of question generation comes from the National Reading Panel (2000), which defined question generation as a type of instruction where readers ask themselves questions about various aspects of the text. Taboada and Guthrie (2006) defined student questioning as self-generated requests for information within a topic or domain. The student or reader, not the teacher, asks the questions. Student-generated questions help to focus readers and promote better reading comprehension or understanding of the written text (Chin, Brown, and Bruce, 2002).

The question-generation strategies in this book pertain to both *narrative* and *informational* text. Both genres tell stories that use imaginative language and express emotion, often through the use of imagery, metaphors, and symbols. Narrative text includes any type of writing that relates a series of events and includes both fiction (novels, short stories, poems) and nonfiction (memoirs, biographies, news stories).

Informational text provides factual accounts of social and natural occurrences. In the last decade, research on the importance of informational text has exploded, based largely on the work of reading researcher Nell Duke. In

Table 1 Inclusion of Text Genres in Common Core State English Language Arts Standards

Grade Span	Percentage of Narrative Text	Percentage of Informational Text
K–4	50	50
5–8	45	55
9–12	30	70

her year-long study of twenty first-grade classrooms, Duke (2000) pointed out an alarming dearth of informational text; during written language activities, students were exposed to only 3.6 minutes of informational text per day. Furthermore, informational text represented less than 10 percent of first-grade classroom libraries.

Informational text engages the reader with aspects of the real world by conveying and communicating factual information. Informational text differs from narrative text in both the content and the structure of the text. Informational text typically has the following characteristics: (a) communication of information about the natural or social world; (b) content that is both factual and durable; (c) timeless verb tenses and generic noun construction; (d) technical or content-specific vocabulary; (e) material to classify and define the topic of interest; (f) text structures including compare/contrast, problem/solution, cause/effect, and enumeration/description; and (g) embedded graphical features including diagrams, indices, charts, and maps (Duke, 2000 and 2004).

Of particular importance, today's Common Core State Standards (2010) emphasize a significant shift to more complex text and to informational text. Prior to the Common Core, students in elementary grades spent the majority of classroom instructional time immersed in narrative text. Table 1 shows the increasing inclusion of informational text across grade levels.

According to the Common Core State Standards (2010), primary grade students should be active readers of nonfiction text, who recall information, construct meaning, and comprehend beyond the literal level.

PROMOTING CHILDREN'S NATURAL CURIOSITY

Any parent or teacher will attest to the sheer magnitude of questions generated by young children. On an average day, mothers typically are asked an average of 288 questions a day by their children aged two to ten (Frazier et al., 2009). Girls aged four are the most curious, with 390 questions per day (Society for Research in Child Development, 2009). Parents field one question every two minutes and thirty-six seconds. Within one year, children have posed 105,120 questions. Chouinard and colleagues (2007) revealed that children ask between four hundred and twelve hundred questions each week!

THE LACK OF STUDENT-GENERATED QUESTIONS IN TODAY'S CLASSROOMS

Though children come to school with a natural curiosity, there unfortunately comes a time when their questions taper off. An interesting quandary arises between young children's innate curiosity and the role of questions in classrooms today: There seems to be little room for student-generated questions in classrooms today. A noteworthy reading researcher, Linda Gambrell, eloquently stated, "On the other hand, students ask few questions."

Children don't suddenly cease to have questions about their expanding world. Instead, there is a shift in who generates the questions; the majority of questions are generated by the teacher, rather than coming directly from students. Research (Leven and Long, 1981) shows that teachers in 1912 spent approximately 80 percent of instructional time asking questions; these findings were replicated seven decades later. Instead of posing questions, the typical school child answers questions—quite a lot of questions. Teachers ask between 300 and 400 questions each day (Leven and Long, 1981). That figure translates into up to two questions every minute, around 70,000 a year, or two to three million in the course of a career.

Though questions abound in schools, these questions are too often generated by the teacher or by the teachers' manual. In her 2001 book, Courtney Cazden studied the use of teachers' language in classrooms. She found that teachers most naturally relied on a language pattern known as "Initiate, Respond, and Evaluate" (IRE). In the three-step IRE process, the teacher initiates classroom talk by posing a question to students. Next students respond to the question, and finally the teacher evaluates the correctness or appropriateness of their responses.

The majority of these questions are low-level questions that focus on lower cognitive skills, such as memorization and factual recall (Wilhelm, 1991). Richard Allington (2014), one of the most prolific educational researchers, called the "interminable number of low-level literal questions" a "misguided but common instructional move" (p. 18). He explained that the "trivial" questions found in teachers' manuals do little to actually improve reading comprehension. Research also indicates that low-level literal questions dominate the commercial reading series prevalent in today's classrooms (Allington and Weber, 1993; Dewitz, Jones, and Heahy, 2009).

However, research indicates the power of effective questions; Taylor and her research team (2000) found that more effective teachers asked five times as many higher-order questions as less effective teachers. Chapter 1 overviews the academic, cognitive, and educational benefits of question generation.

GENERATING QUESTIONS IN THE DAY OF THE COMMON CORE STATE STANDARDS

The ability to generate questions is a high priority in today's classrooms. The Common Core State Standards (CCSS) (2010) emphasize question generation throughout the developmental spectrum of elementary grades. As readers rise in grade level, the questions that they are expected to ask become increasingly complex. Second graders are expected to ask journalistic-type questions (who, what, where, when, why, and how) about explicit information in a text. By the end of fourth grade, students are expected to ask both closed-ended and open-ended questions, requiring both inference skills and critical thinking. As Ciardiello (2012/2013) stated:

> Indeed, the very first standard for reading literature and informational text recommends that students need to be taught with prompting and support to ask and answer questions about key ideas and details in literature and informational text. The standards also require that students ask questions to confirm understanding of silent reading, read aloud texts, and information presented orally or through other media. (p. 15)

According to Ciardiello, good questioning involves both cognitive and metacognitive dimensions. Within the CCSS, students must "question an author's or speaker's assumptions and premises as well as to assess the veracity of claims and the soundness of reasoning" (p. 15). Ciardiello believed that this type of question deals with the cognitive dimension of good student questioning behavior because "it demonstrates an inquiring mind that searches for novel ideas and extends understanding and comprehension" (p. 14). Asking a good question helps the student with college and career readiness.

Table 2 tracks question generation as a developing skill across grade levels in the Common Core Standards.

In early elementary grades, students are expected to generate explicit questions; by upper elementary, students hold the responsibility to generate questions relying on inferences and an author's message.

Even the means by which students' reading proficiency is measured highlights the importance of questioning as a cognitive skill. Under the National

Table 2 Common Core Question-Generation Tasks by Grade Level

Grade Level	Task	Associated CCSS Strand
K	With prompting and support, ask and answer questions about key details in a text.	CCSS.ELA-LITERACY.RL.K.1
1	Ask and answer questions about key details in a text.	CCSS.ELA-LITERACY.RL.1.1
2	Ask and answer such questions as *who, what, where, when, why,* and *how* to demonstrate understanding of key details in a text.	CCSS.ELA-LITERACY.RL.2.1
3	Ask and answer questions to demonstrate understanding of a text, referring explicitly to the text as the basis for the answers.	CCSS.ELA-LITERACY.RL.3.1
4	Refer to details and examples in a text when explaining what the text says explicitly and when drawing inferences from the text.	CCSS.ELA-LITERACY.RL.4.1
5	Quote accurately from a text when explaining what the text says explicitly and when drawing inferences from the text.	CCSS.ELA-LITERACY.RL.5.1

Assessment of Educational Progress (NAEP), students are required to read multiple genres of text and be able to answer questions about their reading. Seventy to 80 percent of the questions on the NAEP require the ability to answer higher-level questions including critique, evaluation, and interpretation. Raphael and Au (2005) noted that only a third to a fourth of the NAEP questions are basic recall questions. Thus, as students are assessed on their ability to answer sophisticated questions, it is logical to teach students to generate such types of questions independently. As explained by Taylor and colleagues (2003), students need instruction on the strategies required to ask and answer challenging questions.

Measuring Teacher Effectiveness According to Classroom Discourse

As the demands of the Common Core State Standards rise, so do the expectations for today's teachers. In a complex system of teacher evaluation, the amount of conversation that goes on in the classroom plays an essential role. Current evaluation systems judge teachers' effectiveness by the discourse between students and teachers.

More specifically, let's look at the criteria used by New York City—the nation's largest public school system—to evaluate teacher performance. Component 3B of the Danielson (2013) framework addresses teachers' use of questioning and discussion techniques. The following indicators show that teachers are expected to include questions of high cognitive challenge, formulated by both students and teachers:

- Questions of high cognitive challenge, formulated by both students and teachers
- Questions with multiple correct answers or multiple approaches, even when there is a single correct response
- Effective use of student responses and ideas
- Discussion, with the teacher stepping out of the central, mediating role
- Focus on the reasoning exhibited by students in discussion, and in give-and-take with both the teacher and their classmates
- High levels of student participation in discussion

In the Framework for Teaching, teachers are held to the following expectation for rich classroom discussions:

> Class discussions are animated, engaging all students in important issues and promoting the use of precise language to deepen and extend their understanding. These discussions may be based around questions formulated by the students themselves. Furthermore, when a teacher is building on student responses to questions (whether posed by the teacher or by other students), students are challenged to explain their thinking and to cite specific text or other evidence (for example, from a scientific experiment) to back up a position. This focus on argumentation forms the foundation of logical reasoning, a critical skill in all disciplines.
>
> Not all questions must be at a high cognitive level in order for a teacher's performance to be rated at a high level; that is, when exploring a topic, a teacher might begin with a series of questions of low cognitive challenge to provide a review, or to ensure that everyone in the class is "on board." Furthermore, if questions are at a high level but only a few students participate in the discussion, the teacher's performance on the component cannot be judged to be at a high level. In addition, during lessons involving students in small-group work, the quality of the students' questions and discussion in their small groups may be considered as part of this component. In order for students to formulate high-level questions, they must have learned how to do so. Therefore, high-level questions from students, either in the full class or in small-group discussions, provide evidence that these skills have been taught.

Thus, an essential element in classroom discourse stems from student-generated questions. As teachers' effectiveness is evaluated on the basis of these rich conversations, student-generated questions serve an essential role.

JUICY QUESTIONS

As teachers and parents, we often find ourselves complimenting students with, "That's a good question." But what exactly qualifies a question as a good one? When Barell (2008) posed this question to fourth- and fifth-grade students, their responses were that a good question meets the following criteria:

- Has more than one answer
- Has a very deep meaning
- Contains exciting words because that makes someone want to look for the answer
- Doesn't have a yes or no answer
- Has more than one answer, and is something you wonder about
- Is hard to answer and takes a lot of thinking to understand the question
- Is about something you can research
- Takes a long time to figure out
- Has meaning and details in the answer and should make sense
- Is one that I keep thinking about but still don't know the answer
- Makes you think, know, and wonder
- Is not one that everybody already knows the answer to (p. 91).

This book primarily focuses on *juicy questions*. Juicy questions are not those answered with a simple "yes" or "no"; they do not have one right answer. They are provocative and engaging. They promote rich conversations and discussions, where students take turns, share their opinions and views, and deconstruct ideas. And perhaps most importantly, they lead to more juicy questions.

THE GRADUAL RELEASE OF RESPONSIBILITY AS A THEORETICAL FRAMEWORK

Underpinning the notion of teaching students to generate questions is Pearson and Gallagher's (1983) work on the *Gradual Release of Responsibility*. Originally developed for reading instruction, the Gradual Release of Responsibility is an instructional framework that shifts the cognitive load from the teacher to the student. This model consists of four purposeful steps, moving from the teacher-as-model, to joint responsibility of teacher and learner, to independent practice and application by the learner:

1. *Teacher modeling (I do—you watch):* Here teachers model their own processes as active readers. The teacher models, explains, thinks aloud, and shows students how to go about a particular skill. Students observe as the teacher holds the primary responsibility.
2. *Guided instruction (We do it):* During guided instruction, teachers prompt, question, facilitate, or lead students through tasks that increase understanding of a particular text. The student and teacher work together to apply the metacognitive strategy. Here, the teacher demonstrates, suggests, and leads.
3. *Collaboration (You do it together):* Here students work together to apply the strategy in new ways. In a group setting, students work collaboratively to practice the strategy. Here the teacher observes, coaches, provides feedback, encourages, and clarifies.
4. *Independent Practice (You do—I watch):* Because of the previous scaffolded instruction, students are now ready to try the strategy independently. Here the teacher assists, evaluates, and responds.

The overall notion of the Gradual Release of Responsibility is to progress in a cyclical and fluid fashion from teachers holding the primarily instructional role to students holding the primary responsibility for their learning. As students hold more responsibility, they can competently and independently apply a new learning strategy. The classroom vignettes in this book illustrate teacher modeling, scaffolded instruction, and guided practice in shifting the responsibility of question generation to students.

CONCLUDING THOUGHTS

We can no longer afford to gloss over the questions that children naturally bring to today's classrooms. Teachers and parents must use the Gradual Release of Responsibility to help students build the academic language to generate juicy questions in multiple text genres. Opportunities abound for teachers and parents to capitalize on the Common Core's emphasis on question generation in multiple text genres. Furthermore, today's teacher evaluation systems measure effectiveness on the basis of the ability to facilitate, scaffold, and moderate conversations initiated by student-generated questions.

Chapter 1

Inside Inquiry-Based Classrooms
The Research Basis for Question Generation

"He who questions much, does and discusses much shall learn much."

—Sir Francis Bacon

Question generation has a long and rich history in education. In fact, question generation can be traced back to the Socratic Method, a form of inquiry and discussion in which learners ask and answer questions to stimulate critical thinking. The 1860 edition of Barnard's *American Journal of Instruction* (see Ross, 1860) stated that "to question well is to teach well."

This chapter has multiple objectives: (a) to define question generation in the realm of inquiry-based classrooms; (b) to explore the research base of question generation; (c) to understand the role of question generation in today's Common Core State Standards; and (d) to trace the taxonomy of questions.

INTELLECTUAL CURIOSITY IN ELEMENTARY CLASSROOMS

When children ask questions, they demonstrate intellectual curiosity. Hynes-Berry (2012) defined intellectual curiosity as "the sense of intrinsically meaningful satisfaction that lifelong learners experience when they discover or understand yet another thing" (p. 23). As curious children ask the "whats," "whys," and "wherefores," they build internal motivation for learning and attach personal relevance to what they learn. Researcher Lillian Katz (2010) posited that intellectual curiosity is innate and inborn and that educators must nurture that quality in children. Harvey and Goudvis (2000) believed that questioning pushes readers forward in making meaning of text. Their 2000 text called for classrooms that celebrate curiosity.

Curiosity spawns questions. Questions are the master key to understanding. Questions clarify confusion. Questions stimulate research efforts. Questions propel us forward and take us deeper into reading. Human beings are driven to find answers and make sense of the world. (p. 81)

This intellectual curiosity is inherently linked to *inquiry*, a higher-level thinking process in which learners seek knowledge, raise questions, search for answers, and evaluate information to seek new understanding (Wallace and Husid, 2011). The crux of inquiry-based classrooms is problem-solving tools to build and extend students' knowledge. Wilhelm (2007) noted that inquiry addresses the following:

- Focusing on essential questions in disciplines
- Connecting to students' background knowledge to what will be learned
- Addressing gaps in understanding by providing new information in relation to what is already known
- Focusing on realistic applications for knowledge being constructed

At the heart of student-generated questions is an instructional model known as *inquiry-based classrooms*. Research exploring the model of inquiry-based classrooms appeared in the 1980s (Jacobs, 1989; Travers, 1998). In inquiry-based classrooms, students' questions and curiosities drive learning, rather than a teacher-directed curriculum. Inquiry-based classrooms focus on questions in an attempt to address real-world questions. The focus is on the relevance and functionality of the topic, rather than rote memorization or glossing over of facts and information. Inquiry-based learning focuses not on the product of learning but rather on the process. With an inquiry-based approach, students develop the skills and dispositions to be lifelong learners.

Research highlights the effectiveness of inquiry-based classrooms. In his 2004 study, Weglinsky demonstrated higher student test scores associated with inquiry-based instruction. Subsequent researchers in multiple disciplines confirmed these findings (McTighe, Seif, and Wiggins, 2004; Ross, Hogaboam-Gray, and McDougall, 2003). In today's classrooms, teachers often cover curriculum and deliver content in a transmission approach. Often referred to as the *information-transmission approach*, this type of instruction is teacher-centered. Decades of research bringing together the fields of cognition and literacy have discredited this approach to classroom instruction. For instance, Ralph Tyler's (1949) work highlighted learning as a student-driven action, explaining, "It is what he does that he learns, not what the teacher does" (p. 63).

THE BENEFITS OF QUESTION GENERATION

The learning benefits of children posing questions are profound. As children pose questions, they engage their higher-level thinking skills. They think critically. They make sense of things—the world around them, the texts they encounter, the experiences they have. They focus on essential information and synthesize their understandings. Questions show our children as engaged and inquisitive. As children generate questions, they learn to not accept information at its face value but instead to extend their learning in a self-directed manner.

The Cognitive Benefits of Question Generation

The field of education and learning has recently undergone a rapid explosion in neuroimaging, an attempt to measure the structure and functions of the brain (Fletcher et al., 2004). Magnetic resonance imaging (MRI) measures blood flow activity in the brain. A 2014 research team from University of California Davis (see Singh, 2014) monitored brain activity to measure how engaged learners were in reading questions and their answers.

When learners' curiosity is piqued by questions and their answers, the parts of the brain associated with pleasure, reward, and creation of memory underwent an increase in activity. These findings indicate that curious brains are better at learning tasks, leading researchers to conclude that "curiosity really is one of the very intense and very basic impulses in humans. We should base education on this behavior."

Question Generation to Build Reading Comprehension

In addition to its cognitive benefits, question generation is highly effective with regard to reading comprehension (Cohen, 1983). For the purpose of this book, reading comprehension is the higher-level cognitive process of making and extracting meaning of a text (Snow, 2002). Reading comprehension is an active, problem-solving process, encompassing "intentional thinking during which meaning is constructed through interactions between text and reader" (Durkin, 1993, p. 5).

Comprehension involves recalling information from text, extracting themes, engaging in higher-order thinking skills, constructing a mental picture of text, and understanding text structure (van den Broek and Kremer, 2000). These metacognitive tasks have led researchers to believe that "the most important thing about reading is comprehension" (Gambrell, Block, and Pressley, 2002, p. 3).

A wealth of research demonstrates the effectiveness of question generation, leading the National Reading Panel (2000) to conclude that "the strongest scientific evidence for the effectiveness of a text comprehension intervention was found for the instructional technique of question generation (p. 4–45)." Question generation aids students with memory, recall, and identification and integration of main ideas through summarization. Students who generate their own questions show improvement in reading comprehension scores; in their meta-analysis of question generation, Therrien and Hughes (2008) reported significant findings for the use of question generation as a way to improve students' comprehension.

Harvard-based reading researcher Catherine Snow (2002) wrote that "teaching students in grades 3–9 to self-question while reading text enhances their understanding of the text used in the instruction and improves their comprehension" (p. 33). Janssen (2002) noted that "self-questioning leads to increased comprehension and more and more high-level questions" (p. 98). Furthermore, question generation holds the reader accountable for "deeper interactions with text" (Tabaoda and Guthrie, 2006, p. 4). When students generated questions, they performed better on tests examining knowledge of story structure than those who did not receive such training (Nolte and Singer, 1985; Singer and Donlan, 1982).

Studies on question generation have examined both expository and narrative text. Davey and McBride (1986) conducted research with fifty sixth-graders to evaluate the effects of generating questions on passage comprehension. Students were randomly assigned to one of two groups: question-generation group and read-reread group.

Each student was given four expository passages to read, at the end of which were eight free-response comprehension questions. After reading the passages and before answering the questions, each group was given different directions. The question-generation group was asked to generate two "think" type questions about the most important ideas of the passage, which made them think about what they had read but which they could not answer directly from text information. Looking back in the text was not permitted. The read-reread group was instructed to read, reread, and study the passage thoroughly before answering the questions. The results revealed that those in the question-generation group performed better on the higher-order inference post questions than those in the read-reread group.

Dreher and Gambrell's (1985) work corroborates these findings; after learning to formulate questions on the main ideas of expository passages, sixth-graders outperformed students who did not learn the strategy in terms of answering main ideas for new paragraphs. Research by Ezell et al. (1992) also demonstrated third-graders' ability to create and formulate their own questions by discriminating between the reader's knowledge base and the text to which the question referred. These students had gains of 2.2 in grade equivalent scores, compared to those who did not receive any questioning instruction.

Question Generation to Build Reading Motivation and Engagement

An additional benefit of student-generated questions is a deep engagement and involvement with text. By posing and answering their own questions, students become more involved with their reading. Grasesser, McMahen, and Johnson (1994) described an active learner as one who shows that inquisitiveness and curiosity. When a student poses questions about text, he or she is "actively involved in reading and . . . motivated by his or her queries rather than those of the teacher" (National Reading Panel, 2000, p. 4–110). This active involvement gives students an initiating role in their learning (Taboada and Guthrie, 2006).

Not only does question generation improve comprehension but self-questioning activities also promote a positive attitude toward reading and literacy (Yopp and Dreher, 1994). Yopp and Dreher (1994) randomly assigned sixth-grade students to two different treatment groups: (a) teacher-generated questioning and (b) student-generated questioning. The students who received instruction on how to generate their own questions were more engaged in literacy instruction, assigned texts, and classroom discourse. Simply put, students are motivated by questioning and finding the answers to their questions (Singer and Donlan, 1989).

UNDERSTANDING THE TAXONOMY OF QUESTIONS

In educational research, multiple approaches to classifying questions exist. Early classification systems grouped questions into two broad categories: (a) lower order, for memory, rote, and simple recall and (b) higher order, for more demanding and exacting thinking. Today's question classification systems hold their roots in 1912 research by Rommiett Stevens, who—in classroom observations—noted that teachers asked approximately 395 questions each day. The majority of these questions, about two out of three, were asked at a low intellectual level, usually requiring little more than rote memory and recall. This body of research indicated that teaching meant talking and asking questions.

Subsequently, researchers and teacher educators set forth to alter these trends. Researchers focused their work on improving the quality of classroom questions and determining the intellectual demands of teachers' questions, leading to the following classification systems. Presented below are the two most commonly accepted questioning classification systems: (a) Bloom's Taxonomy (1956) and its 2001 revision and (b) Gallagher and Ascher (1963).

Bloom's Taxonomy (1956)

Perhaps the most influential classification system comes from Benjamin Bloom. An educational psychologist, Bloom identified the levels of intellectual behavior important to learning: the cognitive (intellectual), psychomotor (physical), and affective (attitudes and emotions). Further, he identified a range of six cognitive levels that reflect the appropriate intellectual activity. These six levels relate to how the brain processes information and are listed below, in order of lowest to highest cognitive demand.

1. *Knowledge:* Requires that students recognize or recall information. Remembering is the key intellectual activity. Includes the verbs *define, recall, memorize, name, duplicate, label, review, list, order, recognize, repeat, reproduce, state.*
2. *Comprehension:* Requires that students demonstrate sufficient understanding to organize and arrange material mentally; demands a personal grasp of the material. Includes the verbs *translate, explain, classify, compare, contrast, describe, discuss, express, restate in other words, review, select.*
3. *Application:* Requires that students apply information, demonstrate principles or rules, and use what was learned. Includes the verbs *apply, classify, solve, use, show, diagram, demonstrate, record, translate, illustrate, choose, dramatize, employ, operate, practice, schedule, sketch, write.*
4. *Analysis*: Requires students to identify reasons, uncover evidence, and reach conclusions. Includes the verbs *identify motives and causes, draw conclusions, determine evidence, support, analyze, deduce, categorize, compare, contrast, criticize, differentiate, justify, distinguish, examine, experiment.*
5. *Synthesis:* Requires that students perform original and creative thinking. Includes the verbs *write or arrange an original composition, essay or story, make predictions, solve problems in an original way, design a new invention, arrange, assemble, collect, compose, construct, create, design, develop, formulate, manage, organize, plan.*
6. *Evaluation:* Requires that students judge the merit of an idea, solution to a problem, or an aesthetic work. Includes the verbs *judge, value, evaluate, appraise, argue, assess, attach, choose, compare, defend, estimate, rate, select.*

As a whole, Bloom's Taxonomy helps teachers to understand the need for high-level skills. As students move up from low-level skills, there is an increase in the likelihood of their retaining information.

Bloom's Taxonomy Revised (2001)

Revised to better meet the learning demands of the twenty-first century, the Revised Taxonomy changed the categories to verb forms to reflect their more familiar use as part of education objectives. The revised categories are Remembering, Understanding, Applying, Analyzing, Evaluating, and Creating.

The biggest difference between Bloom's Taxonomy and the Revised Taxonomy is in the latter's reliance on subcategories. The subcategories provide greater flexibility and responsiveness to the cognitive complexity of the activity. For example, the category Applying requires greater mental activity than Understanding, but "explaining" is a high subcategory of the Understanding category, and "executing" is a low subcategory of the Applying category even though explaining is a more complex activity than executing.

Gallagher and Ascher (1963)

Following up from the original Bloom's Taxonomy, James Gallagher and Mary Jane Aschner developed a widely used system that created four divisions, ranging from simple recall to more difficult thought, to creative thinking, and finally to evaluative thinking. Their hierarchical taxonomy of four different question levels is as follows:

1. *Cognitive-memory* requires only simple processes like recognition, rote memory, or selective recall to formulate an answer. ("Name a novel written by Stephen King.")
2. *Convergent thinking* requires analyzing and integrating data to formulate an answer. There is only one correct answer for questions at this level. ("Which is the better temperature setting for a home freezer: $-2°$ Celsius or $-2°$ Fahrenheit?")
3. *Divergent thinking* requires a response using independently generated data or a new perspective on a given topic. There is more than one correct answer for such questions. ("Write two different equations for which -5 is the solution. One should be a one-step equation, and the other should be a two-step equation.")
4. *Evaluative thinking*, the highest question level in this taxonomy, deals with matters of judgment, value, and choice. ("What should be done to improve our health care system? Explain your answer.")

This taxonomy divides questions into four quadrants with paired criteria; questions are either high or low order and are either convergent or divergent in their design. This classification system was later modified by William Wilen (1991).

Low Order versus High Order. Low-order questions require students to merely recall a single fact, whereas high-order questions demand that the student comprehend the text in relation to a greater context or situation. Let's examine a simple question to see how it can move from low level to high level.

In a second-grade classroom, a teacher reads an informational text about cheetahs. She asks the students, "What color is the cheetah?" With this *low-order* question, the teacher simply checks students' ability to recall a factual tidbit from the text. Student responses are narrowly limited to answers such as tan, brown, and black. Using the same text, a teacher might generate a *high-order* question: "Why might the cheetah's colors be useful?" To answer this question, students must consider the cheetah's colors in relationship to its survival and its habitat.

Convergent versus Divergent. Questions may also be convergent or divergent. *Convergent* questions have a narrowly defined correct answer—one that is short, specific, factual, and requires little reflection from the reader. Convergent questions are close-ended questions; they are answered directly by the text. On the other hand, *divergent* questions are open-ended. They are broader, may have multiple answers, and require a higher level of thinking to generate a response.

A divergent question is answered by elements from the text and the student's analysis and explanation. So in that same second-grade classroom reading a text about cheetahs, a convergent question might be "What other animals rely on their ability to camouflage?" This question involves recall of text or outside knowledge. A divergent question might ask, "What might happen to a cheetah that was born without spots?" This question forces the reader to consider an outside scenario and generate a logical answer based on new knowledge from the text.

Explicit Questions versus Implicit Questions

In 1978, Pearson and Johnson developed a system to clarify questions. Their classification system consisted of three types of questions:

1. Textually Explicit (TE), in which the question and answer are derived from the text and the relationship between the two is explicitly stated

2. Textually Implicit (TI), in which inference is necessary and both the question and answer are derived from the text
3. Scriptually Implicit (SI), in which a question is derived from the text and an answer is reasonable but nontextual in nature.

This early taxonomy was the first to highlight the importance of various types of questions and how they relate to both the reader and the text. The next chapter explores how this taxonomy served as the basis for other question generation strategies commonplace in today's classrooms.

UNDERSTANDING DIFFERENT TYPES OF QUESTIONS

In addition to understanding classification systems, it is essential to understand the major dichotomy between the two key types of questions. Although they have many different names, questions essentially boil down to two different types: *explicit* or *implicit* questions.

Explicit questions have clear and obvious answers; they are often literal or factual. Explicit questions only have one correct answer that generally is answered explicitly in a text. The answers to these questions are transparent. Implicit questions require the reader to draw conclusions and make inferences based on interpretation and deduction. Implicit questions go beyond the text, requiring students to activate their background knowledge and hypothesize potential answers. Implicit questions may trigger discussion, spark debate, and give students the flexibility to be engaged problem solvers.

These two types of questions have several other names in research and various question generation strategies:

- Thin versus thick questions (Harvey and Goudvis, 2000)
- Open versus closed questions (Schuman and Presser, 1979)
- Text-based versus knowledge-based (Scardamalia and Bereiter, 1992)
- In the Book versus In My Head (Raphael, 1984)

Explicit and implicit questions are created under different conditions. Students usually ask text-based questions when studying a text and do so because of certain cues provided to them. By contrast, knowledge-based questions are more spontaneous and based on students' interest or desire to make sense of something. Often, these knowledge-based questions reflect a higher-order thinking process than text-based questions.

In addition, knowledge-based questions require more integration of learned information into previously known knowledge. Scardamalia and Bereiter (1992) found that when students were reading about a less familiar topic such as fossil fuels, they asked questions requiring basic information. However, when the topic was more familiar, students asked more questions of a wondering type, which reflected interest, curiosity, and puzzlement.

Let's consider the following classroom example. Observing a first-grade classroom, Hynes-Berry (2012) watched a teacher read aloud *The Three Little Pigs*. At the conclusion of the story, the teacher asked, "Which of the three little pigs' houses was the strongest?" This closed question leaves little room for debate, provocative conversation, or dissenting voices. On the other hand, let's consider the possibilities that emerge from an open-ended question such as "What might it mean to have a house that is so strong it could not be blown away?" This richer, juicier question engages students in problem solving, builds a connection between the text and the students' personal lives, and helps students construct knowledge and understanding in a meaningful way.

CONCLUDING THOUGHTS

This chapter links question generation to inquiry-based classrooms and highlights the indisputable research proving the multiple benefits of questioning. The different question classification systems and different levels of questions are presented so that teachers and parents understand the need for higher-level questions in today's classrooms and homes. The subsequent chapter examines the use of these classification systems and different levels of questions in tried-but-true question generation strategies.

THINK ABOUT IT

- Evaluate the ideas of an inquiry-based classroom in relation to your teaching. In what ways do you practice inquiry-based instruction? How could you make more space for inquiry-based instruction on a daily basis?
- Looking at the classification systems of questions, what types of questions do you use most frequently in your teaching/instruction?

Chapter 2

Tried-But-True Questioning Strategies

"The absence of comprehension is related to not knowing how to find the questions to ask, or not knowing how to find the relevant answers."

—Smith, 1994, p. 53

Though the objective of this book is to examine innovative ways to encourage student-generated questions, it is important to explore the legacy of questioning strategies with a rich history of classroom application and research. Wilhelm (2007) referred to these as "questioning schemes," which support reading, text-based discussions, and meaning making. This chapter specifically focuses on the following tried-but-true questioning schemes: (a) Question-Answer Relationship (Raphael, 1986); (b) Question Formulation Technique (Rothstein and Santana, 2010); (c) KWL (Ogle, 1986); (d) Reciprocal Teaching; and (e) reQuest (Manzo, 1969).

QUESTION-ANSWER RELATIONSHIP

In the mid-1980s, researchers out of the University of Chicago devised a question-generation strategy known as *Question-Answer Relationship* (QAR) (Raphael, 1984). QAR is primarily a structure to help children classify and categorize questions. Raphael and Au (2005) explained that QAR "gives teachers and students a language for talking about the largely invisible processes" of reading comprehension, and asking and answering questions (p. 208). QAR builds from the categories and terms devised by Pearson and Johnson (1978), who focused on text implicit and explicit questions.

Understanding the Four Types of QAR. Raphael divided questions into two broad groupings titled "In the Book" and "In My Head." To help students see the difference between these types of questions, teachers focus on the sources of information necessary to answer questions. *In the Book* questions can be answered explicitly with information from the text, whereas *In My Head* questions involve the reader's personal connections, background knowledge, and opinions/responses. These two broad categories can be further subdivided into four types of QARs:

1. *Right There* questions have only one answer found explicitly within the text.
2. *Think and Search* questions are also explicit but require the reader to put together different parts of the text in responding.
3. *Author and You* questions require the reader to "read between the lines," using prior knowledge and implicit information to make inferences.
4. *On Your Own* questions relate to a student's life experiences and beliefs and don't actually require the student to have read the text.

Young children may only be ready for the *In the Book* and *In My Head* categories, but by second grade, students can begin to differentiate between *Right There* and *Think and Search* QARs (Raphael and McKinney, 1983). By fourth grade, students can understand the differences among the four core QARs (Raphael and Wonnacott, 1985). Table 2.1 shows the question stems commonly used in QAR.

The Academic Benefits of QAR

Multiple studies have shown the academic benefits of QAR (Raphael and McKinney, 1983; Raphael and Pearson, 1985; Raphael and Wonnacott, 1985). In 1992, Ezell and colleagues showed that low-, average-, and high-achieving third-grade students improved on asking and answering comprehension questions as a result of instruction in QAR. Memsmer and Hutchins (2002) focused their instruction on using QARs to draw students' metacognitive awareness to graphics and charts within a text. Their findings revealed that QAR instruction helped students to analyze text features and to determine how to obtain answers to questions. Similarly, studies have indicated the value of applying the QAR strategy to the illustrations within picture books (Chien, 2013; Cortese, 2003). Jones and Leahy (2006) posited that generating questions facilitates deeper thinking than the process of merely answering questions. In recent work, researchers created a schoolwide literacy project, coaching students on how to analyze standardized test questions according to their QAR classification.

Table 2.1 Question-Answer Response Question Stems.

In the Book	
Right There	Think and Search
What did . . .	How do you . . .
Who did . . .	What happened to . . .
How many . . .	How long did . . .
What was . . .	What time did . . .
Who are . . .	What happened before . . . What
When did . . .	happened after . . . How would you
What does . . .	describe . . . What examples . . .
What kind . . .	Where did . . .
Who is . . .	How do you make . . .
What is . . .	Why does . . .
Where is . . .	Explain . . .
Name . . .	Compare . . .
List . . .	

In My Head	
Author & Me	On My Own
Do you agree with . . .	Have you ever . . .
Why did the main character . . .	What are the reasons that . . .
What did they mean by . . .	If you could . . .
How did she/he feel when . . .	If you were going to . . .
Give reasons why . . .	What are the pros and cons of . . .
What do you think . . .	Do you know anyone who . . .
What if . . .	How do you feel about . . .
What do you think will happen . . . What did the author mean by . . .	What is your favorite . . . why . . .
What did the character learn about . . .	What do you do when . . .
	What can be exciting about . . .
	What do you already know about . . .
	What would you do if . . .

As students identified the type of QAR in a test question, they were more proficient in answering correctly. Its powerful research base led to the following claim:

> QAR provides a responsible approach to preparing students for high-stakes tests at different grade levels and in a variety of subject areas, without detracting from the high-quality instruction that leads to high levels of literacy. (Raphael and Au, 2005, p. 220)

A Classroom Example: QAR with Young Readers

In a second-grade classroom, a teacher familiarizes her students with the four types of questions in QAR. She presents the following text:

Tom has lived in Marysville his entire life. However, tomorrow, Tom and his family would be moving 200 miles away to Grand Rapids. Tom hated the idea of having to move. He would be leaving behind his best friend, Ron, the baseball team he had played on for the last two years, and the big swing in his backyard where he liked to sit and think. And to make matters worse, he was moving on his birthday! Tom would be thirteen tomorrow. He was going to be a teenager! He wanted to spend the day with his friends, not watching his house being packed up and put on a truck. He thought that moving was a horrible way to spend his birthday. What about a party? What about spending the day with his friends? What about what he wanted? That was just the problem. No one ever asked Tom what he wanted.

To reinforce the concept of QAR, the teacher presents students with the following questions. To her, it matters less that the students provide the correct answer to her question; instead, she focuses on their ability to identify each type of question and how they would approach the text to answer each question.

1. How long has Tom lived in Marysville? *Think and Search—You need to know Tom has lived there his whole life and that he is about to turn 13, in order to answer this question correctly.*
2. What is the name of the town where Tom and his family are moving? *Right There—You can point to one sentence to get the answer to this question.*
3. What might Tom do to make moving to a new town easier for him? *Author and Me—Because it asks specifically what would make Tom feel better about moving, the reader needs to consider what she knows about Tom to give him specific suggestions.*
4. Does Tom like playing on the baseball team he has played on for the last two years? *Author and Me—The reader must infer from the passage that Tom enjoys baseball—and decide whether or not he likes playing on that specific team.*
5. In what ways can moving to a new house and to a new city be exciting? *On My Own—The reader doesn't need any information from the passage to answer this question.*
6. What is Tom's best friend's name? *Right There—You can point to one sentence to get the answer to this question.*

Final Thoughts on QAR

As students recognize the four different types of QAR questions, they begin to understand the relationship between questions, the content of narrative and expository text, and the knowledge a reader brings to the page. The strategy shows that students who understand how questions are written are better prepared to answer the questions. These activities help students "demystify" the question-building process as a step toward better reading comprehension. Chapter 8 goes into more depth on using QAR with fifth-graders.

QUESTION-FORMULATION TECHNIQUE

A second question-generation strategy comes from the Right Question Institute, known for creating Question-Formulation Technique (QTF). *Make Just One Change: Teach Students to Ask their Own Questions* organizes learning around the questions that students independently generate (Rothstein and Santana, 2010). QFT follows four basic tenets:

1. Ask as many questions as you can.
2. Do not stop to judge, discuss, edit, or answer any question.
3. Write down every question exactly as it was asked.
4. Change any statements into questions.

More specifically, QFT follows these six steps:

1. *Teachers design a question focus.* The Question Focus is a prompt that can be presented in the form of a statement or a visual aid to hook students, to focus and attract their attention, and to quickly stimulate question asking. The Qustion Focus is not a teacher's question but rather is the springboard for students to identify and explore a wide range of themes and ideas.
2. *Students produce questions.* Students use the aforementioned protocol for producing questions without assistance from the teacher. While working, the rules provide a firm structure for an open-ended thinking process. Students are able to generate questions without being inhibited by judging the worth of each question.
3. *Students improve their questions.* Students then improve their questions by analyzing the differences between open- and closed-ended questions and by practicing changing one type to the other. The teacher leads them through a discussion of the advantages and disadvantages of both kinds of questions.
4. *Students prioritize their questions.* The teacher leads students in prioritizing their questions as they relate to the teacher's learning objectives. Here students move from thinking divergently to thinking convergently and plan concrete action steps for getting information they need to reach their learning objectives.

5. *Students and teachers decide on next steps.* Here, students and teachers work together to decide how to use the questions.
6. *Students reflect on what they have learned.* The teacher gives students an opportunity to review what they have learned by producing, improving, and prioritizing their questions. Making the QFT completely transparent helps students see what they have done and how it contributed to their thinking and learning.

When used in classroom instruction, QFT, as teachers have reported, increases participation in group and peer learning processes, improves classroom management, and enhances their efforts to address inequities in education. The result of QFT is students who can ask deeper, more probing questions in a more timely fashion.

Rothstein and Santana (2014) noted the following about QFT:

> Question formulation promotes student voice and critical thinking. As students learn to produce their own questions, they are thinking *divergently*—that is, more broadly and creatively. When they focus on the kinds of questions they are asking and choose their priority questions, they are thinking convergently—narrowing down, analyzing, assessing, comparing, and synthesizing. And when they reflect on what they have learned through the process, students are engaged in metacognition—they are thinking about their thinking.

Final Thoughts on QFT

As students generate questions, they keep the generative process in forward motion by not evaluating or judging the value of any questions. All voices are honored as all questions are recorded. As students translate statements into questions, they become familiar with the language and phrasing inherent in question generation.

KWL

KWL (Ogle, 1986) is an instructional reading strategy that guides students through comprehending texts before, during, and after reading. This strategy serves many purposes to facilitate reading comprehension; the KWL encourages students to activate their background knowledge about a text, to set a purpose for reading, and to monitor the knowledge they have gained from a text. KWLs have become commonplace in classrooms because of their student-centered approach. KWLs most commonly take the form of a three-column graphic organizer, as displayed in table 2.2.

KWLs are most easily applicable to informational text. Students work on the first two columns before reading a text. In the far-left-hand column, students have to activate their background knowledge by brainstorming everything that they *know* about a topic. This information is recorded in the K column of a K-W-L chart. For younger readers, the teacher may act as a scribe, being careful to record all of the students' reported knowledge regardless of its accuracy.

The second column aligns most closely to the purpose of this book: giving students the power and responsibility for answering questions. In the middle column, students generate a list of questions about what they *want to know* about the topic. These questions are listed in the W column of the chart. It may be useful for teachers to provide students with sentence starters to lend them the academic language needed to generate questions. A student might state, "I want to know what lives in the rainforest." With a bit of modeling, a teacher might redirect that statement into a question. By saying, "Let's rephrase that so it starts with the word *what*," the same student might generate the question, "What lives in the rainforest?"

During or after reading, students answer the questions that are in the W column. This new information that they have *learned* is recorded in the L column of the K-W-L chart. The KWL gives teachers a lot of instructional bang for their buck, meaning that there is little to prepare on the teacher's end for significant comprehension gains before-during-after reading.

A 2015 *Washington Post* article called the KWL "an ingenious teaching tool . . . that is easily corrupted—and often implemented so poorly as to undermine any meaningful benefit." The author (Strauss, 2015) noted that too often in KWLs, teachers write down students' questions and then ignore them, teaching the unit exactly as planned. Instead, the KWL should be used as a framework for "children's questions that actually drive the lesson—as opposed to a list of prefabricated outcomes produced by the teacher, district administrators, or state legislature":

Table 2.2 KWL (Know-Want to Know-Learned) Chart

K	W	L
What I Know About the Topic	What I Want to Know About the Topic	What I've Learned About the Topic

This approach constitutes not just an alternative to the top-down standards-and-testing movement that has come to define "school reform"; it's a rebellion against traditional teacher-centered classrooms that remain the norm in most public and private schools—classrooms where virtually the entire curriculum is devised without any input from the students themselves and without attention to the needs and interests of these particular students.

Inside a Fifth-Grade Classroom: KWL About Rainforests

A fifth-grade teacher is confident that her students have experienced the KWL chart since early elementary school. She believes their struggles lie with the W column—where they think through what they hope to know. She explains the following:

> My students are reluctant to generate questions because they simply don't know where to begin. It's almost like they are overwhelmed in what they don't know—as a result they end up writing only a few questions or writing really simple questions that are narrow in their scope. So I've tried to re-envision having them generate questions that stem directly from what they've told me they already know. It's sort of like we look at what they know and stretch out questions from those statements. Once they realize that questions can piggyback off of what they already know, they've been able to write questions that are better in quantity and quality.

As her students begin a new unit of study on rainforests, she is eager to show them how informational text helps them to act as scientists and researchers. She begins with a KWL chart, giving students three quiet minutes where they brainstorm things that they already know. She records their responses on chart paper. For the most part, their statements are simple: "They have lots of trees." "It rains a lot in the rainforest," and "Animals live in rainforests." However, she uses the K column as a springboard to generate questions; when a student offers the simple statement, "Rainforests are becoming extinct," she leads them in the following conversation.

> *Teacher:* So you're telling me that you already know that rainforests are becoming extinct. But first, remind me what extinct means?
>
> *Students:* (shouts out) Disappearing!
>
> *Teacher:* Yup, when a rainforest is becoming extinct, that means it's disappearing. That's a really important thing to know. We also know that scientists use what they already know to think about things that they still want to know. So let's think through how we could take this sentence that you're telling me

you already know and use it to write a question we hope we learn the answer to. Remember that juicy questions start with the words like "Why?" and "What might." So any ideas on a question we could ask from the statement we already know?

Student 1: Why does it matter that the rainforest is disappearing?

Student 2: What would happen if the rainforest became extinct?

Teacher: Great questions. You add them to your KWL, and I'll add them to our class chart.

In preparation for an upcoming rainforest unit, students generate the following questions:

- Does the rainforest get a lot of sun?
- What kinds of animal and plant species live in the rainforest?
- What kinds of endangered animals live in the rainforest?
- How many species live in the rainforest?
- How does a species in the rainforest become endangered?
- How do people and dangerous animals coexist in the rainforest?
- Why is there so much rain in the rainforest? How often does it rain?
- What kinds of people live in the rainforest?
- Why are trees in the rainforest so tall?
- What would happen if the rainforest disappeared?
- What is the purpose of cutting down trees in the rainforest?

Final Thoughts on KWL

Across decades of instruction, KWL remains popular for several reasons. First, it is easy for teachers to implement and for students to master. It supports students before reading as they activate background knowledge and set a purpose for reading. As they generate questions about the text, they approach it with motivation and concrete goals. In completing the L column, they gain visual evidence of their learning. As a result, the KWL has many great qualities that make it a "must use" in the classroom.

RECIPROCAL TEACHING

Reciprocal Teaching, a means to encourage the simultaneous application of multiple reading comprehension strategies, first appeared in the mid-1980s. The seminal research on Reciprocal Teaching comes from Palinscar and

Brown (1984), who envisioned reading comprehension as being an opportunity for readers to use multiple strategies simultaneously, rather than single discrete strategies. Reciprocal Teaching employs the four strategies of predicting, clarifying, questioning, and summarizing. Oczkus (2010) referred to these strategies as the "Fab Four." Within the Reciprocal Teaching framework, students predict before reading and check the accuracy of their predictions throughout the reading. They clarify sources of confusion, unknown words, or unfamiliar concepts during reading. They take on the role of the teacher to ask questions during and after reading, for the purpose of checking for understanding. After reading, they summarize the key elements and essential ideas of a text.

Understanding the Fab Four Strategies

The uniqueness of Reciprocal Teaching comes not from the reading comprehension strategies themselves but rather from the integration of multiple strategies. An explanation of and a rationale for each of the strategies are given below:

Predicting occurs when students hypothesize what the author will discuss next in the text. In order to do this successfully, students must activate their relevant background knowledge. The students read for the purpose of confirming or disproving their hypotheses. Furthermore, they link new knowledge from a text to their pre-existing knowledge. Text structures (including headings, subheadings, and graphics) aid students in anticipating what will unfold next in the text.

In *summarizing*, students aim to identify and integrate the most important information in the text. Readers summarize across sentences, across paragraphs, and across the passage as a whole. As novices to this instructional procedure, students' summarization efforts focus on the sentence and paragraph levels. As they become more proficient, they integrate at the paragraph and passage levels.

Question generating is a flexible strategy that holds students to ask questions both within and beyond the text. They might generate questions about sources of confusion or unfamiliar vocabulary. *Clarifying* encourages students to be metacognitive, or to monitor their own comprehension. When the students are asked to clarify, they focus on the many reasons why the text is difficult to understand (e.g., new vocabulary, unclear reference words, and unfamiliar and perhaps difficult concepts). They become aware of comprehension breakdowns and to take the necessary measures to restore meaning (e.g., reread, ask for help).

As Strickin (2011) explained, the teacher holds three responsibilities in teaching students to use Reciprocal Teaching:

1. Before reading, activate prior knowledge of concepts and vocabulary.
2. During reading, monitor, guide, and provide assistance for students in employing the Fab Four strategies.
3. After reading, debrief on the activity and lead student reflection in the use of multiple reading comprehension strategies.

In her work with English learners, Williams (2010) teaches *heavyweight* and *lightweight* questions. In heavyweight questions, students move toward higher levels of critical thinking, whereas lightweight questions are more literal and recount information explicit in the text.

The Research Base of Reciprocal Teaching

Across diverse populations and ages, Reciprocal Teaching has demonstrated strong effects in research (Coley et al. 1993; Kelly, Moore, and Tuck, 2001; Myers, 2005; Palincsar and Brown, 1984). Reciprocal Teaching has been heralded as effective in helping students improve their reading ability in pre-post trials or research studies. Reciprocal Teaching has been found to be beneficial for students with learning disabilities (Kettman-Klinger and Vaughn, 1996). These students improved their reading skills despite being poor comprehenders. Reciprocal Teaching can also be used in a higher-education setting, as college students can struggle in understanding complex readings, such as scholarly articles and historical texts (Doolittle et al., 2006). Westera and Moore (1995) used three groups of students (those who received Reciprocal Teaching for a short period of time, those who received Reciprocal Teaching for an extended period of time, and the control group, which did not receive Reciprocal Teaching). Over a five-week period, the students in the extended time Reciprocal Teaching group increased their reading comprehension scores more than one age-equivalent year. In this study, 95 percent of the extended Reciprocal Teaching students showed gains in comprehension, compared to 47 percent of students in the short Reciprocal Teaching group and 45 percent of the students in the control group.

Final Thoughts on Reciprocal Teaching

Though it is not commonplace in classrooms today (Williams, 2010), there is clear evidence highlighting the effectiveness of Reciprocal Teaching. Although Reciprocal Teaching is a difficult strategy for teachers to incorporate into their lessons, reports have consistently shown that it is the most effective way to engage readers with texts. Students report that they read and understand more when they use Reciprocal Teaching than when they read text independently (Fisher, Frey, and Williams, 2002). This approach—incorporating multiple strategies—teaches students to determine important ideas from a reading while discussing vocabulary, to develop ideas and questions, and to summarize information. It can be used across several content areas; it works particularly well with textbooks and nonfiction text.

reQuest

The author of reQuest (Manzo, 1969) claimed his strategy was the first to help students develop "an active, inquiring attitude." Developed in his doctoral dissertation and then explored in language arts journals, reQuest aims to move student-generated questions from literal to implied, eventually resulting in the development of critical questioning skills. The strategy is intended to help students to re-envision the types of questions that they generate, or "re-question" a text until they can answer questions with higher-level thinking. In reQuest, students create three kinds of meaning while they read:

- *On the lines*, where students recognize factual information that is directly stated in a text
- *Between the lines*, where students make connections in text details or connect their experience to a text in order to make inferential moves
- *Beyond the lines*, where students extend their thinking beyond a text to evaluate it and apply it to the larger world

The steps to teach reQuest are quite straightforward, as outlined below:

1. Both teacher and students read the title and first sentence only of the first paragraph of a selection, and look at any pictures or graphics that are part of the introduction.
2. The teacher tells students to ask as many questions as they wish about the first sentence, the title and/or pictures, or graphics. The teacher turns his or her copy of the selection face down, but students may continue to look at their copies. Students are encouraged to ask the kinds of questions that they think a teacher might ask.
3. When all student questions have been fully answered, the teacher turns his/her book face up while students are instructed to turn theirs face down. The teacher then asks as many additional questions (about the title, first sentence, and illustrations) as seems appropriate to bring about a sense of focus and purpose for reading the selection. The last of these questions (on the first sentence, and then in subsequent question sets on following sentences) should simply be, "What do you suppose the remainder of this selection will be about?"

4. The next sentences are handled in the same way, with the students again leading off the questioning, followed by the teacher questioning, and concluding with the question, "What do you suppose the remainder of this selection will be about?" The number of sentences covered should be based on teacher judgment: The ReQuest activity should conclude as soon as a plausible purpose for reading has been evolved but should not last more than about ten minutes.
5. At the conclusion of the ReQuest activity, the student is encouraged to continue reading the selection silently for the purpose that has been developed.
6. Following silent reading, the teacher should first ask the evaluative question: "Did we read for the right purpose?"

Final Thoughts on ReQuest

Though reQuest does not have a significant research basis, it assists students in overcoming their tendency to conclude only what they have predicted. It also focuses students on incorporating effective strategy instruction into their independent reading. Finally, it promotes the metacognitive habit of monitoring one's own comprehension and use of strategies while reading.

CONCLUDING THOUGHTS

These five strategies have been reviewed to trace the history of question generation in educational research. All of these strategies offer research validity, proving their effectiveness with students of diverse ages and backgrounds. In the following chapters, these strategies are reintroduced or reviewed as they are modified and applied in classroom applications.

THINK ABOUT IT

- Evaluate your familiarity with these tried-but-true questioning strategies. Which ones have you incorporated? Which ones might you want to try? What are the strengths and weaknesses of each strategy?
- Research points out a discrepancy between the effectiveness of Reciprocal Teaching and the scarcity with which it is employed by classroom teachers. Why do you think this is so? Why are more teachers not incorporating Reciprocal Teaching?
- Evaluate the role of questions across all of these tried-but-true strategies. Does each strategy incorporate questioning for the same purpose/reason?

Chapter 3

Questioning Inside Kindergarten Classrooms

"How many of your students know how to ask persistent and urgent questions of their own?"

—Dan Rothstein and Luz Santana, 2010

OVERVIEW

This chapter highlights how even our youngest children can generate complex questions. Young children often start their questions with wondering statements, or what Barell (2008) calls *wonder talk*. Judith Lindfors (1999) identified some of the common wondering statements that young children shared in informal discussions:

- There's a part I wanted to ask about . . .
- I'm trying to figure out . . .
- This is what I don't get . . .
- I thought it was . . .
- I wonder why . . .
- Maybe . . . perhaps . . .

Highlighted are two strategies: (a) changing *notices* and *text connections* into *wonderings* with hand symbols and (b) picture walks in narrative texts. These classroom vignettes showcase creative opportunities to give young children the academic language and cognitive capabilities to generate questions.

Kindergartners in Context

For many young children, kindergarten is the first formal schooling experience and the longest block of time spent away from their parents and/or caregivers. In kindergarten, students follow class rules and social norms, such as cooperating with other students, taking turns, and sharing materials. From a literacy standpoint, students recognize and write letters of the alphabet in both uppercase and lowercase form. They also begin to recognize sight words such as *the*, write consonant-vowel-consonant words such as *bat* and *fan*, and read simple sentences.

More specifically, the Common Core State Standards hold kindergartners to the following English Language Arts reading expectations:

- With prompting and support, ask, and answer questions about key details in a text
- With prompting and support, retell familiar stories, including key details
- With prompting and support, identify characters, settings, and major events in a story
- Ask and answer questions about unknown words in a text
- Recognize common types of texts (e.g., storybooks, poems)
- With prompting and support, name the author and illustrator of a story and define the role of each in telling the story
- With prompting and support, describe the relationship between illustrations and the story in which they appear (e.g., what moment in a story an illustration depicts)
- With prompting and support, compare and contrast the adventures and experiences of characters in familiar stories
- Actively engage in group reading activities with purpose and understanding

CHANGING NOTICES INTO WONDERINGS WITH HAND SYMBOLS

Young children struggle with the academic language needed to generate questions. They are unsure of the grammatical structures and the signal words used to generate questions; they are stuck in asking their questions in sentence form (e.g., "I want to know where the cat goes.")

Children need support in acquiring the language skills needed to generate meaningful questions. Outlined here is a scaffolded process to help young readers turn statements into notices, notices into questions, and questions into wonderings. This process leads to student questions from independent, skillful readers who use noticing, connections, and wonderings as tools for comprehension and reflection.

Noticing

Five-year-olds notice everything, for better or worse. They notice tiny details, from the color of the carpet to the teacher's tiny pimple. A veteran teacher of twenty years capitalizes on his kindergarten class's power of observation with familiar books.

At the beginning of the school year, he digs out fairy tales and other familiar and comfortable picture books. Because children do not struggle with unfamiliar plots or characters, their read-alouds become more of a discussion. Students share out what they notice in the read-aloud. Animated dialogue ensues as children admonish Red Riding Hood for not listening to her mother. They giggle at Rumpelstiltskin's funny clothing. The teacher focuses on these statements and rephrases them as *notices*:

> Did everyone hear what Julia said? She said Rumplestiltskin is wearing funny clothing. Julia made an interesting notice. Everyone take your finger and gently touch the tip of your nose with them, like you are honking a horn. When a reader notices something he says, "I notice that" and touches his fingers to his nose. Let's try it together.

In this way the teacher easily connects the symbol to the skill. Within a few short days, read-alouds are peppered with nose taps and declarations of notices.

Once the young readers appropriate this symbol, the teacher discusses the difference between *simple notices* and *deep notices*. In his second reading of a familiar text, he pushes students to be more observant:

> Let's try something a little more challenging—a deep notice. (The teacher taps his nose). I notice the daughter's face is scared on this page. This is a deep notice. It isn't easy to spot. You have to be an observant reader to see this.

Children rise to the challenge of linking noticing to a physical symbol. This instruction is inherently differentiated as readers of all levels can make simple or deep notices. The following days are filled with nose tapping and discussions about whether a notice is simple or deep. The groundwork for creating connections from these notices, and eventually questions or wonderings, has been laid through simple and deep noticing.

Connecting

After a few weeks of simple and deep noticing, the teacher introduces connections. The most developmentally appropriate connection for five-year-olds is a text-to-self connection. The teacher starts by making a simple

Figure 3.1   Noticing Symbol

notice in a familiar read-aloud. One of his favorite books for this purpose is Mo Willem's (2004) *Knuffle Bunny: A Cautionary Tale*.

In this book, the main character, Trixie gets her favorite stuffed animal, Knuffle Bunny, mixed into the wash at the Laundromat. On her way back home, Trixie realizes she is missing Knuffle Bunny. Being unable to use her words, she throws a classic toddler tantrum. When they arrive home, Trixie is hysterical and her dad is perplexed. Mom immediately recognizes the problem and the family sprints back to the Laundromat. They dig through the dryer and discover the missing bunny, prompting Trixie to say her first words, "Knuffle Bunny."

The teacher uses this familiar tale to immediately teach personal connections to literature. He demonstrates another hand symbol in this way:

> Trixie and her family live in the city. I live in the city too. I just made a text-to-self connection (he holds his hand in the shape of a C to his chest and repeats). Trixie lives in New York City and I live in New York City. Let's try this new symbol. Everyone make the letter C with your hand and hold it to your chest. A text-to-self connection is when something in the story reminds you of something in your own life.

He prompts children to look for any text-to-self connections they can make. With this symbol, the teacher encourages all different levels of text-to-self connections, easily meeting the varied academic levels of the readers. Some children make more abstract text-to-self connections while others sustain concrete connections. One child reports his text-to-self connection that, like Trixie, he does his laundry in a Laundromat. All text-to-self connections are accepted and celebrated for their value.

On a subsequent reading of the same book, the teacher increases the level of abstractness of these connections. A second reading includes a text-to-self connection that connects Trixie's favorite Knuffle Bunny to the teacher's favorite childhood stuffed animal, FuFu Bear. He brings his hand in the shape of the letter C to his chest and says, "When I was Trixie's age, I had a favorite stuffed animal called FuFu Bear. I carried it everywhere like Trixie carries Knuffle Bunny everywhere. It made me feel safe. Huh. I wonder if Trixie feels safe with Knuffle Bunny." With this last line, the teacher gives the first foreshadowing of wonderings. He hints at the use of connections to develop questions about the characters and the story.

When the readers apply these connections with ease and in conjunction with simple and deep notices, the teacher moves on to introduce text-to-text connections. For this task, he selects a follow-up book: *Knuffle Bunny Too: A Case of Mistaken Identity* (Willems, 2007).

38   Chapter 3

Figure 3.2 Connections Symbol

   The second in the *Knuffle Bunny* series finds Trixie in pre-K, still clutching her beloved stuffed animal. She and her friend accidently swap almost identical Knuffle Bunnies at school. Only at bedtime do both she and Sonja realize the error of mistaken identity. After a late-night exchange of bunnies at a neighborhood playground, the girls return happily to bed.

The teacher holds up this new book and revisits some of the familiar hand symbols:

> Let's start with the cover. Look (tapping his nose with the notice symbol) I notice Trixie! I have a connection. It's not a text-to-self; it's different. I make the same symbol (he holds his hand in the shape of a C to his chest), but this time I am connecting a text-to-a text. I have a text-to-text connection. In the first *Knuffle Bunny* (he holds the book up with his right hand) there is the character of Trixie and her Knuffle Bunny. In our new book, I see Trixie and her Knuffle Bunny on the front cover too (the teacher holds up the second book in his left hand). Something that happened in one book reminds me of something that happened in another book.

The next day the teacher continues text-to-text connections by introducing the third book in the Knuffle Bunny series: *Knuffle Bunny Free: An Unexpected Diversion* (Willems, 2010).

In this third book, Trixie embarks on an airplane trip to visit her grandparents with her Knuffle Bunny. Trixie forgets Knuffle Bunny on the plane and makes it through a whole week Knuffle Bunny-free. On the plane ride home she is reunited with Knuffle Bunny, only to give it up to comfort a crying baby in the row behind her. Trixie leaves the plane, grown-up and no longer in need of Knuffle Bunny.

Students and teachers offer many text-to-text connections, shuffling between the three books, connecting characters and even emotions. Students are entertained by the familiar and consistent texts and make text-to-text connections with the author, characters, setting, and feelings.

It is with these familiar texts and the Knuffle Bunny books that students have acquired multiple reading strategies. Following the modeling of the teacher, these students can apply the skill of noticing to the physical symbol of simple and deep notices. Simple and deep notices are extended to incorporate text-to-self connections and text-to-text connections. These connections are also named, defined, and given a physical symbol. Weeks of preparation and groundwork have led to the introduction of wonderings.

Wonderings

To introduce wonderings, the teacher introduces the readers to one of his favorite authors, Tomie DePaola. He begins with *Strega Nona* (1975), warming up with familiar notices and text-to-self connections.

A Caldecott award winner, this picture book tells the story of an Italian witch doctor who is known for her successful remedies. She cures headaches, rids people of warts, and plays matchmaker for the single women in her town.

As she gets older, she employs the assistance of a young man named Big Anthony who "didn't pay attention." He secretly observes her singing a spell to a magic pasta pot to produce large amounts of cooked pasta; unfortunately, he fails to notice that she blows kisses to the pot three times to stop the pasta production.

When Strega Nona leaves on a short trip, Big Anthony attempts to summon humongous amounts of pasta for the villagers. As he does not know how to stop the pot, a great sea of noodles overflows across the town. Upon returning home, Strega Nona blows kisses three times, and the town is saved. Saying "the punishment must fit the crime," Strega Nona hands a fork to Big Anthony and commands him to eat all the pasta he has conjured.

The teacher introduces two new hand symbols:

> Today I'm going to show you two special signs that we will use to help us ask questions. We will use three fingers on one hand to make the letter "W." "W" will stand for the word "Wonder." Wonder is what you say when you want to find out something. Wondering helps you to ask questions. Watch as I make my pointer finger, my middle finger, and my ring finger point tall to the sky, and I pinch my thumb and my pinky finger behind them. It's the same way you show the number three on your hand. In our class, this special hand symbol means, "I wonder." We will use it every time we have a question about a book we are reading, every time we want to know something.

As the children practice making the "I wonder" symbol with their hands, the teacher continues his explanation:

> Sometimes there are questions that are easy to answer. We can find their answer right in the book. We will call these questions *simple wonderings*. Let me show you how to make the hand sign for simple wonderings. You take your hand in the shape of the letter W, and you hold it up to your nose. Let's try making the sign for simple wonderings.

The teacher returns to looking at the cover of *Strega Nona*. Touching his nose, he says, "I notice that there is an old lady with an apron, a bunny, and a peacock on the cover." He then transforms the symbol from notice to wonder with the language, "I wonder what this book is about." He lists this question on the top of a chart paper. The teacher elicits responses from the children, modeling the transformation from notice to wonder or connection to wonder. He lists their questions on the chart paper:

- I wonder who the guy on the cover is.
- If *nona* means grandma, I wonder if that is her grandson.
- I wonder if she lives in the country.

Figure 3.3 Simple Wonderings Symbol

- I wonder if she is really a witch.
- Where is Italy?

As he reads the book, he poses more simple wonderings. He checks to see that the children have automatically picked up on the modeled behavior and are holding their fingers up to their noses in the shape of a W. He records all wonderings as they slowly read through the rest of the book. After they finish reading *Strega Nona* for the first time, they leave the list of wonderings for the next reading workshop.

At the beginning of the next reading workshop, the class looks over the list of wonderings. They discuss and practice the symbol for simple wonderings. The teacher reads the list of wonderings to the class and says:

> Let's reread *Strega Nona* and see if we can get the answers to any of the wonderings we had yesterday. As we come to any answers for the questions on our list, let's stop reading and cross off the question that was answered. The book itself can answer some of your questions, either in illustrations or in the text. Let's look at Joe's question—Will Big Anthony try to use the magic pasta pot? (The teacher taps his nose with his fingers and continues.) This picture here shows him repeating the words he hears Strega Nona say over the magic pasta pot. So, the answer to Joe's wondering is yes. We used the book to answer this simple wondering.

As some of their questions go unaddressed, the teacher introduces *deep wonderings*, questions that go beyond the scope of the text. This hand symbol mirrors the previous one, only here he moves his hand—still in the shape of a W—from his nose to his chest.

He explains that "looking at the pictures or reading the book cannot answer some of our wonderings. Sometimes the question goes beyond the text; we will call this a deep wondering. Here is the symbol we will use for a deep wondering." Students mimic him by making the deep wonderings hand symbol. Deep wonderings require the reader to dig deeper in the text to address the question; a deep wondering might require the reader to probe into a character's motivation or to draw inferences about a character's emotions.

The teacher challenges his students to identify any deep wonderings among their list of questions. He directs their attention to the questions on their original list that they did not cross out. They hold deep wonderings symbols up to their chests as they discuss if witches really exist, why Big Anthony never listens, where Calabria is located in Italy, and if there really is such a thing as magic. These deep wonderings plant the foundations for the implicit questions that require a reader to search for information beyond the book.

Independent Application of the Hand Symbols

Now confident that the children can apply these hand symbols with comfort and ease, the teacher turns their attention to the academic language of questioning. The teacher displays the picture book *Roller Coaster* by Marlee Frazee (2006).

Questioning Inside Kindergarten Classrooms 43

Figure 3.4 Deep Wonderings Symbol

Roller Coaster begins with illustrations of a long line of people at a fairground. Ahead of them is a roller coaster named "Rocket." As the line creeps slowly, anxious passengers get out of line. At long last, twelve passengers climb into the cars. Some of them are excited while others appear calm and collected. The illustrations depict the riders as they experience a variety of twists, turns, and loop-de-loops. The passengers react in different ways.

Feeling ill, the tough guys clutch their stomachs and have queasy looks on their greenish faces. A smitten couple snuggle closer as the ride goes on. The elderly couple in the straw hats adore every wild minute; they hoot and cheer as the roller coaster plummets. A little girl in the front becomes a roller coaster enthusiast by the end; she has a huge smile on her face. At the conclusion of the wild ride, the passengers disembark; the little girl insists on riding the coaster one more time.

The teacher explains that he has selected this book because he knows that the class is excited about the upcoming opening of a local amusement park. He displays the cover, which shows a car full of roller coaster riders plummeting down a steep drop, with open mouths and wide eyes as if they are screaming. He holds up the simple wondering symbol and thinks out loud with a simple wondering—"I wonder what this book is about?" Students call out simple notices and make the appropriate symbol: "It's about people on a roller coaster" and "It's about a ride that goes superfast." Holding up the simple wonderings hand symbol, the teacher restates their observations in question format. He transforms the statement of "The people look like they are having fun on the roller coaster" to a question: "Does everyone have fun on a roller coaster?"

Turning to the first page, he reads the line, "All of these people are waiting in line for the roller coaster." He turns to the class, modeling the simple wonderings sign and poses more questions: "I wonder where this roller coaster is." "I wonder how these people are feeling about going on the roller coaster." "Can anyone help me figure out how those wonderings could be turned into questions?" He calls on a boy who mirrors his simple wonderings and responds, "How do they feel about riding the roller coaster?"

As he reads on in the book, he poses more simple wonderings; the pictures depict riders of all ages, prompting him to ask, "Can anyone ride a roller coaster?" "Do you have to be a certain age?"

When he sees that children have automatically picked up on the modeled behavior and are holding their fingers up to their noses in the shape a W, he opens the floor to their questions. He records their answers exactly as they come, some in question form and others in the "I wonder" structure:

- How many people can go on the roller coaster?
- How long do they have to wait?
- I wonder if they can wear their hats on the roller coaster.
- I wonder how fast the roller coaster goes.

By the end of the book, his students have demonstrated the simple wonderings symbol and contributed to the list of questions:

- How does a roller coaster stay on the track? Does it ever fall off?
- What makes a roller coaster so noisy?
- Do you wear seatbelts on a roller coaster?
- Why do people put their hands in the air on a roller coaster? Aren't you supposed to hold on?
- I wonder why those riders are kissing in the back of the roller coaster.
- I wonder why that man is walking away from the roller coaster. Did he decide not to ride?
- How do you get to be a roller coaster ride operator?
- Why can't she open her eyes on the roller coaster?
- Why are most people dizzy after a roller coaster ride?
- I wonder if anyone threw up after riding.
- What do wobbly knees feel like? I wonder how a doctor might fix wobbly knees.

In the second reading, students are able to differentiate between simple and deep wonderings. They use illustrations to count up the number of riders on a roller coaster, they learn about the height restrictions on riders, and they confirm that—just as in a car—roller coaster riders wear seatbelts. They hold deep wonderings symbols up to their chests as they discuss the speeds of roller coasters, why one character appears to have "chickened out" from riding, the job training of roller coaster operators, the typical behavior of roller coaster riders, and the basic mechanics of roller coasters. Though they are not able to satisfactorily answer any of these questions, they are all confident that these are deep wonderings that require a reader to do more than simply reread.

One could easily envision how the simple and deep wonderings stemming from a read-aloud might open up an entire unit of study: additional research into the physics of roller coasters, the history of roller coasters, how force impacts the human body, etc. These symbols provide students a physical cue and the academic language to generate thin and thick questions (see chapter 2). In their construction of deep wonderings, children start to make connections to other books, connections to themselves as people and readers, and connections to their lives beyond the classroom walls.

As they add *simple* and *deep wonderings* to their skill box of effective reading strategies, the wonderings and the symbols take off in the classroom. The W sign is held up to noses and chests during science, math, and writing instruction. The W sign, simple and deep, permeates the staple of early childhood classrooms: the morning meeting, when students wonder, "I wonder why Joe didn't help clean up the blocks" and "I wonder if pillbugs really poop squares."

The deep wonderings produce valuable thinking and enrichment opportunities beyond the prescribed curriculum. Additionally, the simple and deep wonderings build a rudimentary understanding of classifications of questions. By naming wonderings, giving a symbol for them and gradually introducing them to the curriculum, teachers can make the natural wonderings of kindergartners and the questions they generate enrich daily classroom instruction.

GENERATING QUESTIONS DURING A PICTURE WALK

Teachers and parents frequently show children the cover picture of a book and ask them to make predictions about the story based on the cover illustrations. This activity is often referred to as a *picture walk*, a shared activity between an adult reader and a child before reading an unfamiliar story. A picture walk encourages the reader to preview the pictures in a storybook and make predictions about the text. It familiarizes the young reader with the setting, characters, and events of a book, while simultaneously sparking in him or her an interest in the story. Picture walks help children to connect with the visual images in the story so that they can connect the pictures with their own experiences and activate any relevant background knowledge. Additionally, picture walks introduce new vocabulary to a child so that the story can be read with more fluidity and fewer breaks for explanations. Picture walks are easy for parents and teachers to facilitate, following these steps:

- Hold the book so the child can see the cover. Read the title aloud.
- Tell the child that this book has words and pictures, and that right now you're going to look at just the pictures and try to guess what's happening in the story. This is called a "picture walk" because you're going to walk through the pictures in the book without reading the words.
- Take a look at the cover and give the child a chance to take a look as well. Provide a model for the child by describing what you see in the picture. For example, "in this picture, I see a mama bear and her little bear cubs having a picnic."
- When the child is ready to try it on his or her own, ask him or her to describe what he or she sees happening on this page, just as you did. Encourage him or her to speak in sentences and to give as many details as possible.
- Continue to ask the child what he or she thinks the story will be about, based only on what he or she sees.
- Provide vague responses that do not give away any of the story, such as "That's very possible?" "What makes you think that?" and "Are you sure about that?" These responses will help sow the seeds for enthusiastic conversation during the actual reading.
- Slowly flip through the book, page by page, without reading a single word. Ask the child questions about each picture, and try to elicit responses that

require him or her to make inferences based upon the images. The following prompts may be a helpful starting point:
- **What** is going on here?
- **Who** is this?
- **How** might this character feel in this part of the story?
- **When** is this story taking place?
- **How** do you think the story is going to end?

The overarching purpose of the picture walk is to facilitate language interaction between the child and the adult. Not only do picture walks encourage oral conversation, but they also improve students' comprehension as they become actively engaged readers prior to the actual reading.

In the traditional model of a picture walk, the adult is responsible for generating questions to ask to children. As such, the adult facilitates the majority of the conversation, rendering the child responsive to the adult's prompts. With a simple shift, this dynamic can change to one where children generate questions about the images in the text.

In the following example, a teacher uses text images for students to generate questions about the images from the text. Prior to this lesson, the kindergartners had rudimentary understandings of essential elements of fiction text, including characters, setting, and sequencing. Her aim in this lesson is for students to predict the outcome of a story using picture clues.

She selects the children's picture book, *My Friend Rabbit* by Eric Rohmann (2007). Written for beginning readers, the book tells the story of mischievous Rabbit, who gets Mouse's brand-new airplane stuck in a tree. In an effort to dislodge the airplane, Rabbit tugs, drags, carries, and cajoles a wide variety of animals to stand one on top of another under the offending tree. Mouse just reaches the wing of his plane when the entire group comes crashing to the ground. The text of *My Friend Rabbit* is simple:

> My friend Rabbit means well. But whatever he does, wherever he goes, trouble follows. "Not to worry, Mouse! I've got an idea!"/The plane was just out of reach. Rabbit said, "Not to worry Mouse. I've got an idea!"/So Rabbit held Squirrel, and Squirrel held me, but then. . . ./The animals were not happy./But Rabbit means well. And he is my friend./Even if whatever he does, wherever he goes, trouble follows.

Much of the story is told through the illustrations, offering a perfect opportunity to use a picture walk as a means to generate questions. The teacher gathers a small group of children on the rug in front of her, and holds up the cover of *My Friend Rabbit*. Students look at the cover, which depicts a cartoonish rabbit holding a toy airplane against a bright blue sky. A small mouse is nestled in the cockpit of the airplane.

She explains, "This story is about a mouse that is friends with a rabbit. Somehow this rabbit always gets into trouble. Today is a special day because before we even read the book, you get the chance to ask any question you'd like." She points to sentence strips in a pocket chart, displaying the question prompts "How? Who? Why? What? Where? When?" She continues, "Remember that good questions start with these words. I'm going to give you a silent minute to think of some questions, and then I'd like you to turn and talk to your neighbor to share some of the questions that you'd like to ask just by looking at the picture on the cover."

After a brief silence, students murmur their questions while the teacher circulates to eavesdrop on their conversations. She returns to the whiteboard and calls on students to share out their questions. Students eagerly raise their hands to share out their questions. She reminds them that they can ask any questions they think of, and she writes each one on the board to validate their question-generation efforts.

As students are quite familiar with making predictions, they initially resort to their comfort zone and offer predictions based on the cover art. The teacher reminds them that their job is to ask questions, and she adeptly coaches one student on how to convert her statement of "I think that the mouse is driving the plane" to the question "Who is driving the plane?" When a boy states, "I think the bunny is the main character because he's much bigger than the mouse," the teacher poses, "How could we rewrite that prediction as a question that we hope the text answers for us?" She models her thinking, and reports, "What I hear you asking is, 'Who is the main character?'"

The following are the questions generated from these kindergartners:

- Who is driving the plane?
- Where is the plane going?
- What is the name of the bunny?
- What is the name of the mouse?
- What is going to happen in the story?
- What happens in the beginning, middle, and end?
- What is the setting of the story?
- Is this story nonfiction or fiction?
- How is the bunny feeling in the picture?
- Why is the mouse sitting in the plane?
- Who is the main character?

The teacher flips through the book page by page, only showing the illustrations. She reminds the class that they are on a picture walk and that their job is to ask as many questions as they can from the illustrations. From a picture depicting the rabbit holding up an airplane, a student asks, "How much does an airplane weigh?" Another picture shows a rabbit lifting an alligator, a goose, and a bear, prompting a student to ask, "Are rabbits really strong?" When the illustration's orientation changes—forcing the reader to change the book from horizontal to vertical—a student poses, "Why did they draw the picture like that?"

Having generated these questions, students begin the book eager to search for the answers. Much like the vignette of the teacher who taught simple and deep wonderings, some of their questions are addressed in the text and others go beyond the text. The book does not address the likelihood of finding all these characters living together harmoniously or the makeup and physics of airplanes; these kindergarten students will need other texts and other resources to address all of their answers.

CONCLUDING THOUGHTS

The vignettes in this chapter showcase how our youngest readers can build the academic language necessary for question generation. As noticings become wonderings, these wonderings transform into questions. A simple visual cue assists students in the academic language of asking questions—in simple texts or merely with the text's illustrations.

THINK ABOUT IT

- How do you use the illustrations of a text in your read-alouds with children? What is their purpose? How do they support comprehension? How might you use them as a means to facilitate question generation?
- How do you help young children build the academic language necessary to ask questions?
- What foundational skills (cognitive/language/comprehension) do young children need to have in order to generate questions?

Chapter 4

Questioning Inside First-Grade Classrooms

"The ability to routinely generate mental questions while reading, listening, or viewing something not only boosts attention and alertness, but also strengthens comprehension. . . . When you ask yourself questions about incoming information, you are paying attention, self-monitoring, and actively constructing knowledge."

—Lewin, 2010, p. 1

In first-grade classrooms, questions abound as children are naturally curious. This chapter follows several classroom teachers as they generate questions in traditional picture books and informational text. This chapter focuses on the following activities to promote question generation: (a) using simple nursery rhymes to generate complex questions; (b) Probable Passage (Wood, 1984); and (c) informational text walks. These strategies and activities show that skillful readers ask questions before they read, as they read, and after they read.

FIRST GRADERS IN CONTEXT

Perhaps no other grade presents as many literacy milestones as first grade, when most children truly become readers. According to the NAEYC, in first grade, students develop the following foundational literacy skills:

- Reading and retelling familiar stories
- Using strategies (rereading, predicting, questioning, contextualizing) when comprehension breaks down
- Using reading and writing for various purposes on their own initiative
- Orally reading with reasonable fluency

- Using letter-sound associations, word parts, and contexts to identify new words
- Identifying an increasing number of words by sight
- Sounding out and representing all substantial sounds in spelling a word
- Writing about topics that are personally meaningful
- Attempting to use some punctuation and capitalization

More specifically, the Common Core State Standards hold first graders to the following English Language Arts reading expectations:

- Ask and answer questions about key details in a text
- Retell stories, including key details, and demonstrate understanding of their central message or lesson
- Describe characters, settings, and major events in a story, using key details
- Identify words and phrases in stories or poems that suggest feelings or appeal to the senses
- Explain major differences between books that tell stories and books that give information, drawing on a wide reading of a range of text types
- Identify who is telling the story at various points in a text
- Use illustrations and details in a story to describe its characters, setting, or events
- Compare and contrast the adventures and experiences of characters in stories
- With prompting and support, read prose and poetry of appropriate complexity for grade 1

GENERATING COMPLEX QUESTIONS FROM SIMPLE TEXT

The following example comes from a first-grade teacher in a suburban New York school; she believes that teaching questioning techniques is a sometimes difficult—but often necessary—task. To increase her students' ability to generate text, she incorporates an iconic simple text into her instruction: nursery rhymes.

Nursery rhymes are traditional poems or songs for young children. Their usage dates from the late eighteenth/early nineteenth century in Britain; the Mother Goose Rhymes appeared in the mid-1700s. Beyond the sheer enjoyment factor, there are many educational reasons to use nursery rhymes with young readers. As Fox (2001) stated, "if children know eight nursery rhymes by heart by the time they're four years old, they're usually among the best readers by the time they're eight." Below are some of the commonly accepted justifications for the role of the use of nursery rhymes with young readers:

- Nursery rhymes build oral reading comprehension, or the child's ability to listen to a text and make meaning of it.

- Nursery rhymes introduce uncommon vocabulary words, like *fetch* and *pail* in "Jack and Jill."
- Because they are short and easy to repeat, nursery rhymes often serve as some of children's first sentences.
- Because nursery rhymes usually follow a pattern, they help children to recall and memorize.
- Nursery rhymes follow a simple narrative structure, with a beginning, a middle, and an end. Understanding simple sequencing improves children's comprehension.
- Nursery rhymes introduce alliteration the rythm of language ("Goosie Goosie Gander"), onomatopoeia ("Baa Baa Black Sheep"), and imaginative imagery. Children hear these rhymes and act out what they imagine the characters are doing.

Though they appear to be simple text, nursery rhymes serve as a fruitful springboard for our youngest readers to generate complex questions, as showcased by this first-grade teacher.

In her classroom, students have spent several lessons focusing on the simple narrative story structure: They are able to listen to a story and identify the *who, what, where, when, why* and *how* of a story. As their confidence in story structure grows, the teacher uses these skills to teach "I Wonder" stems. The "I Wonder" stems help children to generate questions; they build their knowledge of how "I wonder who this story is about?" is really another way to pose the question, "Who is this story about?"

Beginning with a familiar nursery rhyme, she models the questions that she might ask about a text, as seen below with the nursery rhyme "There Was an Old Woman Who Lived in a Shoe."

There was an old woman who lived in a shoe.
She had so many children, she didn't know what to do;
She gave them some broth without any bread;
Then whipped them all soundly and put them to bed.

With the text projected on the board, she models her "I wonder" language:

As I read that nursery rhyme, there are a lot of things that I wonder. First I wonder why this woman lives in a shoe. I wonder whose shoe it is. I wonder why she chose a shoe to live in, instead of something like a box. I wonder exactly how many children she has. I wonder if they were all her children; were some of them nieces and nephews and grandchildren or even foster kids? I wonder how old all of these children are. I want you to watch as I write out some of my wonderings into questions. Because we've used the who, what, where, when, why, and how format, I'll start my questions with those prompts.

She lists the following questions on the board.

- Who are the children? All hers? Nieces/nephews/grandchildren, foster children? Are they twins or triplets?
- Who owns this shoe?
- What ages are all of the children? If there are so many, does she remember all their ages?
- What are the names of the children? If there are so many, does she remember all their names?
- What is the job of this woman?
- Where is this shoe? In the city? In a field?
- When does she put them all to bed? Is it nighttime, or is she just so tired that she makes them go to bed before it is dark?
- Why does she whip them? Did they misbehave?
- How does she get money to feed all the children? Does she send any of the children out to work?
- How does she get this shoe? Was it abandoned somewhere? Did she buy it somehow?
- How do the children react to being whipped and put to bed?

After sharing out her questions, the teacher reminds students that the text does not always give answers to all of her questions, explaining, "Sometimes readers think beyond the text to answer their questions."

Moving on to the guided practice phase, she displays a nursery rhyme on a large chart paper along with an accompanying illustration next to each stanza. She reads the nursery rhyme aloud. For fluency practice, she incorporates echo and choral reading. She asks students to think of a question they might have about the rhyme, and jots it down on the chart paper. The class generates the following questions, using the nursery rhyme "Humpty Dumpty."

Humpty Dumpty sat on a wall
Humpty Dumpty had a great fall
All the king's horses
All the king's men
couldn't put Humpty back together again.

- How did an egg get on the wall?
- Did he roll out of his house?
- Are his insides all over the ground now?
- How could the horses help? With their hooves?
- Did someone push Humpty off the wall?
- Why does he have legs if he is an egg? Why does he wear pants if he is an egg? (referring to the illustration)

- Where was the king?
- Did the men bring him to a hospital?
- Could they glue his shell back together?

A few days later, she follows the same protocol using "Jack and Jill" as the text.

Jack and Jill went up the hill
To fetch a pail of water.
Jack fell down
And broke his crown
And Jill came tumbling after.

In collaborative practice, the class generates the following questions:

- Was there a well at the top of the hill?
- Why did they have to get water from the top of the hill? Didn't they have water in their house?
- Did Jill push Jack?
- Were they running after each other?
- Why was he wearing a crown?
- Is the crown they are talking about his head?
- Did they get hurt?
- Did the water spill all over them?
- Are Jack and Jill brother and sister?
- Are they friends?
- Who sent them to get the water?
- Where are their parents?

In examining questions from both "Humpty Dumpty" and "Jack and Jill," students recognize that some of their questions are answered through the text and illustrations; for the inferential and critical questions, discussions of their background knowledge or experiences provide possible answers. As the questions abound and increase in complexity, these students develop their ability to question; this essential comprehension skill allows the readers to make a deeper, more thoughtful connection to the text they read.

USING PROBABLE PASSAGE TO GENERATE QUESTIONS

First developed in 1984, Probable Passage (Wood, 1984) encourages metacognitive readers to make predictions, to activate background knowledge about a topic, to make inferences, and to form images about a text. As modified by Beers (2003), Probable Passage requires a teacher to scan a text and select key words and/or phrases in a text. Those words (usually around ten to twelve words) rest in a Word Bank.

The teacher leads a brief conversation to ascertain that students understand the meaning of each word, and then encourages students to arrange the words into categories according to their relationship to the story. The teacher begins by modeling her thinking processes in sorting a few key words into the appropriate categories. Students sort the words into the following categories: characters, setting, and problem. She gradually turns the responsibility over to students to sort the words. It is essential that students understand that there is no right or wrong answer. As they activate background knowledge and make predictions about word usage in an upcoming text, they are touching upon several key reading comprehension strategies.

Other teachers add a category for "Unknown"; this category serves as a repository for the words that stump readers or that don't logically fit into one category. Many teachers intentionally stack the deck with an unfamiliar vocabulary word that students place into the "Unknown" box. This maneuver motivates readers to discover the word's meaning and usage in the text. After reading, they are able to move the "Unknown" word into its appropriate category.

In the typical early-elementary classroom, readers might be ready for five to seven words sorted into three categories. As students become familiar with the activity, become more proficient readers, or mature in grade level, they might be able to sort ten to twelve words into five boxes. Students in upper elementary grades may be ready for an open sort, where they group words as they see fit into logical categories; the teacher does not give them pre-assigned categories.

With a few easy adaptations, Probable Passage can shift into a meaningful question-generation activity. Let's take a closer look at a first-grade classroom, using the popular children's book *Miss Nelson Is Missing* (Allard, 1977). In this classic story, the students in Room 207 misbehave and show no respect for their good-natured teacher, Miss Nelson. Exhausted by their antics and poor behavior, Miss Nelson takes matters into her own hands.

The next day, in place of Miss Nelson, the children meet Miss Viola Swamp. Miss Viola Swamp is short-tempered and impatient; she immediately whips the students into shape and overloads them with homework. Soon after the arrival of Viola Swamp, the children yearn for the lovely Miss Nelson. Unfortunately, no one seems to be able to find her, including Detective McSmogg. Finally, Miss Nelson comes back and is pleased to see an immediate improvement in the class's behavior. Only the telltale black dress hanging in Miss Nelson's closet suggests that there may be more to the class's transformation than initially meets the eye. A perennial favorite for back-to-school, *Miss Nelson Is Missing* requires readers to make inferences and opens conversations about classroom norms.

In a first-grade classroom, the teacher has previewed the storybook and pulled out the following words to begin the Probable Passage activity:

- misbehaving
- story hour
- spitballs
- secret
- meant business
- police
- terrible
- lovely change
- rude
- "You'll be sorry"
- witch

The words are written on large pieces of sentence strips, which hang in the pocket chart at the front of the room. On the whiteboard is a large piece of poster board displaying the Probable Passage activity. The teacher leads the class by explaining the directions and the objective of the activity:

> I'm not going to tell you the title of the story we are about to read. I'm not going to show you the cover of the story. Instead I'm going to share with you some words that come directly from the story. I'm going to use what I already know about the story and about the words themselves to try to put them into the boxes that I think they fit into during the story. It doesn't matter if I'm right or wrong about how I sort the words, because I'm making a prediction. What matters more is that I can explain why I put each word into each box.
>
> Behind me you will see the boxes that I need to sort the words into: I have a box for "Setting"—I guess those will be words about where and when a story takes place. I have a box for "Characters"—I will use this for words that have to do with the people or animals in a story. I have a box for "Problem"—what goes wrong in the story. And I have a box for "Solution"—how the story is resolved or how the problem is solved.
>
> I want you to listen as I try the first few on my own. Then it will be time for you to help me. When I think you're ready, I want you to try some on your own. Let's start with "story hour." I chose this one because I think it goes into the "Setting" box. "Story hour" tells me about a time that takes place, and time has to do with the setting—where and when a story happens.

The teacher picks up the "story hour" card and tapes it onto the chart under the "Setting" box. In her next demonstration, she deliberately chooses a word that does not fit so obviously into one category.

Watch me try the word "police." There's lots of ways this one can go; remember there's no right or wrong answer. It just matters that I can explain the thinking behind where I move each word. So, I know "police" are people, so I could put the word into the "Character" box since the character box is for the people in the story. But "police" are often called when there is a problem—like when something dangerous is happening or something has gone wrong. So maybe "police" goes in the "Problem" box? I also know that "police" are people who help solve problems, so I could also move this word into the "Solution" box since maybe the "police" are a part of how the problem is solved. For now, I think I will put "Police" into the "Character" box. But now I'm even more excited to find out how the word is used in the story. I've got another purpose for reading: to find out how the word "police" fits into this story.

The teacher follows a similar protocol for one more word, modeling her thinking as students silently watch. She then shifts responsibility to them to help her with the next few words. She calls on a few students to explain their rationale for moving "spitballs" into the "Problem" box. One group of students is confident that "misbehaving" goes into the "Character" box, while the remainder of the class places it in the "Problem" box. The teacher breaks up the debate by noting, "Misbehaving seems to be a real question for us. Where does this word go?" The teacher leads the class in sorting the remainder of the words, leaving only one seemingly obvious word ("witch") behind.

As she seems confident that the students are ready for independent practice, the teacher directs them to turn to a neighbor and discuss the best place for the word. Students turn and talk, eventually directing the teacher to move "witch" to the "Character" box as they predict that the witch is likely a character in the book.

When this teacher-directed activity is complete, all of the words have been sorted; the teacher is ready to move onto the question-generation portion of the pre-reading activity. She reminds the class that readers ask questions about texts before they read, while they read, and after they read, explaining the following:

> Just from looking at some words from this book—the words that were in our word bank and the words we just sorted—we can ask some questions. When I look at these words, some questions pop into my head. For example, let's look at the card "You'll be sorry". I've got lots of questions about that. I know from those quotation marks that someone is saying those words—a character is saying to another character, "You'll be sorry." But I wonder who is saying "You'll be sorry"? Who are they talking to? What are they sorry about? I just asked three questions from one short phrase.

Now that she has modeled question generation from a text phrase, the teacher shifts to a guided practice portion and directs, "Let's try one together."

She holds up the word "witch" and prompts, "What questions come to mind about this word—witch?" As students list questions, she records them on a chart paper:

- Who is the witch?
- What does the witch do?
- What does the witch look like?
- Is it a good witch or a bad witch?
- Does this witch have a broom and a black cat?

Continuing with collaborative practice, she distributes the Word Bank phrases to small groups and asks them to think about questions as a group. She circulates to encourage students to generate questions that they hope will be addressed in the text. After five minutes, the teacher facilitates a whole-class conversation as each group shares out its questions. She probes for more questions using open-ended prompts such as, "Can you say more about this?" and "How might we come up with another way to ask that?"

By the end of this fifteen-minute activity, the following questions fill up the chart paper.

The creative use of Probable Passage illustrates how a purposeful reading comprehension activity can be tweaked to encourage question generation. As these readers set a purpose for reading and think about what they already know in relation to a new text, they become more focused in their reading. The activity also motivates readers to check whether the words were used in the text as they had predicted prior to reading. With teacher assistance, students understand how predictions easily transform into questions.

GENERATING QUESTIONS FROM INFORMATIONAL TEXT FEATURE WALKS

The previous chapter explored the use of *picture walks* in narrative texts as a means to generate questions. This strategy can be easily adapted for informational text, an area of particular emphasis in the Common Core. Though having children walk through a text's pictures prior to reading is commonplace in fiction text (Stahl, 2004), this practice is rarely used with informational text (Kelley and Clausen-Grace, 2008). These researchers adapted the picture walk to a *text feature walk*. This strategy helps students to understand how the text features in informational text support comprehension; just as the pictures help a reader while navigating fiction texts, the charts, diagrams, titles and subtitles, and typography support readers in making sense of informational text.

Table 4.1 Questions Generated from Probable Passage for *Miss Nelson Is Missing*

Word Bank Phrase	Questions Generated from this Phrase
Secret	What is the secret? Who kept the secret? Did anyone find out the secret? Is it okay to keep secrets? Why was the secret important?
Meant business	Who "meant business"? What does "meant business" mean? Why did someone mean business?
Misbehaving	Who was misbehaving? Were they punished for misbehaving? What were they doing to misbehave? Why is someone misbehaving?
Spitballs	How do you make a spitball? Who is spitting spitballs?
Police	Did someone call the police? Why? Do the police arrest anyone? Are there cops and robbers?
Story hour	What happens during story hour? Who is reading? Who is listening? Does story hour happen at school? At the library? At home? What story is being read?
Lovely change	What is the lovely change? How does the lovely change happen? Who changes?
Rude	Who is being rude? Were they punished for being rude? What were they doing to be rude? Why is someone being rude? Do they know how to be polite?
You'll be sorry	Who says "You'll be sorry"? Why will they be sorry? Do they apologize?

    For his guided reading session with six students, the teacher selects *Butterflies of the Sea* (Swartz, 2009), which provides information about sea slugs. He purposefully chooses a topic that is largely unfamiliar to students; their limited background information on the topic of sea slugs allows them to generate more questions than a topic with which they are quite familiar. His intent is to encourage students to generate questions from the unfamiliar features of informational text. He distributes copies of the book to each student and asks them to look at the cover. He reads the title and prompts his students:

> The title of this book is *Butterflies of the Sea*. Let me ask you a question about the title, and then we will walk through this book so that you can ask your own questions. Here's my question for you: Do you think there can be butterflies in the sea? Thumbs up if you say no.

Three-quarters of the students put their thumbs up, and he calls on one student to explain her thinking. She explains, "There can't be butterflies in the sea because butterflies live in the air."

He continues, "Thumbs up if you think there can be butterflies in the sea." He calls on another student, who reports, "Butterflies could use their wings to fly in the ocean." The teacher tells his students that this book is about sea slugs:

> Our job is to look through this book and ask questions from its special features. We will look at the pictures, the titles, the different colors and charts. The author and illustrator have used these features for a specific reason, so before we read, I will lead you in asking questions from the different parts of the book. Watch how I use the title to ask a question. I told you that this book is all about sea slugs, but the title is *Butterflies of the Sea*. That brings a question to my mind: Why are sea slugs called "butterflies of the sea?" Do you think there are butterflies in the sea? So now let's walk through this informational text. I will point out its special features before we start reading, and let's try to think of as many questions as we can from the parts of the book.

Beginning with the table of contents, he reminds the students:

> The table of contents gives us an overview of what the parts of this book will be. It is a road map of what we will find in the book. It gives us hints about things we will read in the book, and it is also a great way to ask questions about what we might learn in the book. Let me show you how I use the table of contents to ask questions.

The table of contents outlines these categories:

- About Sea Slugs
- How They Swim
- Their Mollusk Family
- Small Wonders
- Where They Live
- How They Hide

- How They Feel
- How They Breathe
- The Spanish Dancer
- Butterflies of the Sea

He models question generation from the table of contents:

The table of contents tells me that page seven is about "Their Mollusk Family." I have some questions about that. What is a mollusk? Who is in a sea slug's family?

He continues by focusing on how headings both relay information and can be a source of questions:

I see the heading "How They Swim." That tells me that this page will give me information about how sea slugs swim. But that's a juicy place for me to ask a question. I want to know this: How do slugs swim? Do they have wings?

He follows a similar protocol with the typography in the informational text.

As I read I notice these words in dark bold type. That tells me that these are important words about sea slugs. The author wants me to know what these words mean, so he puts them in the glossary at the end of the book. I have questions about these words. The first bold word I see is *flap*. What is a flap? Why does a sea slug have flaps? Where do I find a flap on a sea slug?

He points out how the pictures in this informational text both convey information and can be a source of questions.

In informational texts, we have these glossy color photographs that show me real-life pictures of the book's topic. Since I've never seen a sea slug in real life, I'm curious about what they look like. What does a sea slug look like? The small print under the picture is called the caption, and I can look at the caption for both questions and answers. On page four, this caption tells me that this is called a yellow-skirted slug. I have questions about them. Since there are yellow-skirted ones, are there sea slugs of every color? Where are the slug's eyes? What about its mouth?

He distributes individual copies of the text to each reader, as well as a question booklet—a simple stapled book of lined paper where students can record their individual questions. He reminds students of the questioning guidelines:

Your job in our question booklets is to come up with as many questions as you can. To do this, we are going to look at the features of today's book *Butterflies of The Sea*. I'd like all of you to generate at least three questions in three quiet minutes—the questions that the title and the cover of the book make you want to ask. I want you to practice writing questions about the pictures, the headings, and any other features that you notice.

Students set to work and scribble down their questions stemming from the cover. For the next five minutes, students flip through their individual books and jot down the following wonderings in their question booklets:

- Why do sea slugs have different patterns, and colors?
- Why do they call them *butterflies* of the sea?
- Why don't sea slugs have shells?
- Why are sea slugs squishy?
- What would happen if sea slugs went on land?
- Why are some orange?
- Why are some purple and yellow?
- Are sea slugs yummy when you eat them?
- How can sea slugs swim?
- What do sea slugs eat?
- How are sea slugs small wonders?
- How are sea slugs soft?
- Why do sea slugs lay a lot of eggs?
- Do sea slugs swim slowly?
- How do sea slugs feel?
- How do they see?
- Why do they hide?
- Are they slimy?
- Why are they small?

After asking these questions, students are eager to peruse the text in search of answers. They find the majority of answers to these questions. The question, "How are they soft?" goes unanswered, and the students conclude that additional research is needed to answer this.

At the conclusion of this activity, the teacher prompts students to jot down their new knowledge from this text. He provides them with the sentence starter, "From this book, I learned." As students complete the task individually, he peers over their shoulders and notes that their responses are far more detailed than their often bland and non-descriptive responses. "I learned about sea slugs" is replaced by "Sea slugs stay very still on rocks" and "I learned that crabs and lobsters eat sea slugs." In this classroom, a text feature walk has helped students tap into their inquisitive natures and to increase their retention of this informational text.

CONCLUDING THOUGHTS

First grade is an important time to encourage question generation in classrooms. As children transition to full-day, more academically rigorous classroom instruction, their natural curiosity may dwindle. These three question generation strategies highlight that questions can come from a variety of text: simple nursery rhymes, isolated portions of text as in Probable Passage, and the specialized features in informational text.

THINK ABOUT IT

- Think about the texts you read on a daily basis—emails, magazines, popular fiction, user manuals, etc. How do the text features in these genres help you as a reader? How might you generate questions from them?
- Select a text that has photos (such as a magazine, a newspaper, a manual). Try generating questions solely about the pictures. Keep a log of these questions and reflect on the process of generating questions through images.

Chapter 5

Questioning Inside Second-Grade Classrooms

"I think, at a child's birth, if a mother could ask a fairy godmother to endow it with the most useful gift, that gift should be curiosity."

—Eleanor Roosevelt

As second graders become more adept in navigating diverse text genres, their questions may increase in complexity. This chapter highlights question-generation strategies in picture books, small groups, and biographies. Included are the following activities: (a) "I Wonder" journals; (b) the Question Matrix; and (c) K-W-L-S, a modification on the K-W-L strategy (see chapter 2). These strategies promote question generation before, during, and after reading.

SECOND GRADERS IN CONTEXT

The second-grade reader is building his/her skills in decoding and fluency. Decoding is the ability to become more adept at using patterns to decipher unfamiliar words. Fluency is the ability to read quickly and accurately, a skill that many second graders have developed by the end of the school year. In second grade, students explore the many ways to spell common and less common long-vowel patterns. As they increase their ability to decode multisyllabic words, second graders move from laborious decoding to attacking unfamiliar words by patterns. They decode regularly spelled two-syllable words with long vowels (e.g., *table, because, spider, open,* and *music*) and words with common prefixes like *un-* (e.g. *unlock, unhappy*) or *re-* (e.g. *redo, retell*), and use base words they know, such as *add*, as a clue to decoding new words, such as *addition* or *additional*.

They are expected to read from increasingly more complex text, with particular attention to informational text. Second-grade students improve their ability to process information and concentrate on the task at hand. They make connections between concepts, allowing them to compare and contrast ideas.

More specifically, the Common Core State Standards hold second graders to the following English Language Arts reading expectations:

- Ask and answer such questions as *who, what, where, when, why,* and *how* to demonstrate understanding of key details in a text
- Recount stories, including fables and folktales from diverse cultures, and determine their central message, lesson, or moral
- Describe how characters in a story respond to major events and challenges
- Describe how words and phrases (e.g., regular beats, alliteration, rhymes, repeated lines) supply rhythm and meaning in a story, poem, or song
- Describe the overall structure of a story, including describing how the beginning introduces the story and the ending concludes the action
- Acknowledge differences in the points of view of characters, for example by speaking in a different voice for each character when reading dialogue aloud
- Use information gained from the illustrations and words in a print or digital text to demonstrate understanding of its characters, setting, or plot
- Compare and contrast two or more versions of the same story (e.g. Cinderella stories) by different authors or from different cultures
- By the end of the year, read and comprehend literature, including stories and poetry, in the grades 2–3 text complexity band proficiently, with scaffolding as needed at the high end of the range

"I WONDER" JOURNALS

"I Wonder" journals are adapted from Barell's (2008) use of inquiry journals; he noted that "one of the best ways I know of to become aware of my own inquisitiveness has been to keep my own journals." An "I Wonder" journal is a log of readers' wonderings, inquiries, and observations that lead to question generation. Though often used for higher-level, more metacognitive students, the following vignette highlights how the strategy can be modified for younger readers.

In a charter school in East Harlem, a teacher incorporates "I Wonder" journals during her poetry unit. Already familiar with the basic conventions of poetry, she selects the poem "Honey, I Love" by Eloise Greenfield. Published in 1978, this poem is written from the viewpoint of a young narrator. The narrator loves visits from her cousin, with his Southern accent, his whistling habit, and his swagger. She loves hot summer days when her neighbor Mr. Davis cools off children with a hose. She loves laughing at her paper doll creations with her friend. She loves car rides to the country in her uncle's crowded car. She loves church picnics with delicious food. She loves kisses from her mother. Of all the things in her life, the only thing the young girl does not love is going to bed. The crux of the poem is the simple things that mean the most, like sharing laughter with a friend, taking family rides in the country, and kissing her mama's arm. The poem reminds readers that love can be found just about anywhere.

Before the teacher reads the poem aloud, she encourages students to listen for its rhythm. She distributes their "I Wonder" journals—simple folders with blank pages with the sentence starter "I Wonder" and a graphic of a thought bubble. She uses the title to think aloud (see Ness, 2014) as a means to showcase her thought processes.

> The title of this poem makes me think all about love. But I wonder if it is a love letter from someone to the person that they love. What do they love? Who do they love? All of these questions belong in my "I Wonder" journal.

As some of her young students are not yet writing independently, she allows them to express their questions in illustrations. A student draws a picture of a young girl. The teacher stoops next to her and whispers, "Tell me about this picture. How does it show your question?" The child reports that the picture is the speaker in the poem, and tells the teacher she wants to know what the character looks like, particularly what color her skin is. Acting as her scribe, the teacher uses a blank "I Wonder" page and writes, "What does the girl look like?" "What color is her skin?"

The teacher reads each stanza of the poem, aloud, making sure to stop and to allow children to note their questions in their "I Wonder" journals. She uses a variety of approaches to encourage these questions; sometimes students turn and talk to a neighbor about their questions, sometimes she calls on the whole group to share out their questions, and she also leaves independent time for them to write on their own. At the conclusion of the poem, she scans their journals and notes the plethora of questions:

- How old is the cousin? What do they like to do on his visit? How long does he visit?
- What does it mean when it says "words just kind of slide right out of his mouth?"
- Can you really tell where someone is from by how they talk?
- Why is the word "love" in all capital letters in the middle of the poem?
- How do you learn how to whistle?
- Why does she love the way her cousin walks? Does he walk funny?

- Can the sun really "stick to her skin"? Does that just mean she's hot?
- Who is Mr. Davis?
- Does this take place in the summer?
- Where does this girl live?
- Why does Mr. Davis turn on the hose? Is there a fire? Is he watering plants in the garden?
- Does it feel good when the "water stings her stomach" or does it hurt?
- What is a flying pool?
- Who is Renée? Is Renée a boy or a girl? How old is Renée?
- Why does Renee's doll not have a dress? Does she not have money to buy clothes for her doll?
- How does she make a dress out of paper?
- Does it hurt Renee's feeling when the narrator laughs at her doll?
- Why do they laugh so hard?
- How many people are in her uncle's crowded car?
- Where is the car going? Where is she sitting?
- Why do the church folks like to meet in the country? What do they do there?
- Who are the church folks?
- How does her mama feel when the girl kisses her arm?
- Why is the girl trying not to cry? What does she want to cry about?
- Who is this girl speaking to? Who is the "you" in the final line?

Upon concluding the poem, the teacher asks for volunteers to share out the questions in their journals. A rich conversation ensues, as some of their questions are addressed by the text and others prompt talk where students attempt to answer questions with their personal and real-world knowledge. When one student questions, "Where does this girl live?" her classmate answers, "I think she lives in the city, because it sounds like all the church folks meet in the vacation as a little vacation."

For the remainder of the school year, students return to their "I Wonder" journals as they approach other text genres. They add questions to their "I Wonder" journals during science class and on their field trip to a farm. Based on science texts he sends, one student writes the following questions in his "I Wonder" journal:

- Why do trees and plants grow?
- When was the earth made?
- Why do we walk on two legs?

For any unanswered question, the teacher directs them, "Go jot that down in your 'I Wonder' journal." Teachers might help students by giving the following prompts for their "I Wonder" journals:

1. Questions I have about today's lesson
2. Something I have learned today
3. Some thought-provoking incident in class today.

To extend the idea of "I Wonder" journals, a teacher might use this space for written dialogue back and forth from teacher to student. As students ask questions in their journals, the teacher might answer them—an idea explained in chapter 7.

THE MODIFIED QUESTION MATRIX

As evidenced in the Common Core reading expectations, second graders are building their proficiency with the academic language of question generation. An effective instructional approach to building students' proficiency with the *who, what, where, when, why,* and *how* language comes in the form of the Question Matrix.

The Question Matrix is a visual cueing chart, developed by Chuck Weiderhold (1991). More specifically, the Question Matrix is a set of twenty starters that ask *what, where, which, who, why,* and *how*.

The questions in the top rows of the matrix probe for knowledge and information; those in the lower rows require analysis, synthesis, and evaluation. Stems 1–12 generate literal questions, stems 13–24 generate inferential questions, and stems 25–36 generate evaluative questions. The thirty-six questions can be broken down into three main categories to help students understand the purpose of their questions: (a) questions written in the present and past

Table 5.1   Original Question Matrix

		Event	Situation	Choice	Person	Reason	Means
To check what I know or need to understand I can ask . . .	Present	What is	Where/ When is	Which is	Who is	Why is	How is
	Past	What did	Where/ When did	Which did	Who did	Why did	How did
To learn more about it I can ask . . .	Possibility	What can	Where/ When can	Which can	Who can	Why can	How can
	Probability	What would	Where/ When would	Which would	Who would	Why would	How would
To challenge my thinking I can . . .	Prediction	What will	Where/ When will	Which will	Who will	Why will	How will
	Imagination	What might	Where/ When might	Which might	Who might	Why might	How might

tense that help students to check for understanding; (b) questions written for possibility and probability that help students set a learning goal beyond the text; and (c) questions written for imagination and prediction that challenge students' thinking about a text.

On a cold February morning, a suburban classroom is decorated in red hearts for the upcoming Valentine's Day holiday. Paper-bag mailboxes line the shelves, waiting to be stuffed with Valentine's Day cards. As her students gather on the rug for a read-aloud, the teacher explains, "In honor of Valentine's Day, we are going to read a book about all of the different kinds of love." She shows a Google image of a chinstrap penguin and asks, "Where do you think this penguin might live?" Students rely on their background knowledge from the popular movie *Happy Feet* to suggest that this penguin lives in the cold Antarctic. They are delighted to find out that this penguin actually lives very close to their school—in the Central Park Zoo. The teacher displays the bestselling children's book *And Tango Makes Three* (Richardson and Parnell, 2005) written for readers aged four to eight.

Based on a true story about a nontraditional penguin family living in New York's Central Park Zoo, *And Tango Makes Three* tells the story of Roy and Silo, two male penguins, who are "a little bit different." They cuddle and share a nest like the other penguin couples. When all the others start hatching eggs, they too want to be parents. Determined and hopeful, they bring an egg-shaped rock back to their nest and start caring for it. A watchful zookeeper decides they deserve a chance at having their own family and gives them an egg in need of nurturing. The dedicated and enthusiastic fathers hatch a baby chinstrap penguin, named Tango.

Before reading, the teacher directs students that they will be responsible for asking questions during and after reading. Because the original Q-Matrix can overwhelm students with both the number of questions and its associated higher-level thinking skills, she relies upon a modified Q-matrix. This modified version (table 5.2) has a reduced number of questions (twenty as opposed to the original thirty-six) and provides more assistance in directing students to generate questions about the events, characters, reasons, and results.

During reading, the teacher stops four times to model how to use each box of the modified Q-matrix to generate questions. In the following explanation, she models using the "What is" stem from the event column:

> The text says, "The animals make families of their own. There are red panda bear families, with mothers and fathers and furry red panda bear cubs.... There are toad families, and toucan families, and cotton-top tamarin families too." This makes me wonder about what makes a family a family. I will use the

Table 5.2 Modified Question Matrix

Event	Person/Group	Reasons	Results
Complete these four questions about the event in the text.	*Complete these four questions about one or more of the characters.*	*Complete these four questions about the reasons behind the event.*	*Complete these four questions about the results of the actions taken or the event.*
What is . . .?	Who is . . .?	Why is . . .?	How is . . .?
What did . . .?	Who did . . .?	Why did . . .?	How did . . .?
What will . . .?	Who will . . .?	Why will . . .?	How will . . .?
What might . . .?	Who might . . .?	Why might . . .?	How might . . .?

"what is" sentence starter to ask the question, "What is a family? What makes a family a family?"

In the first column of the modified Q-matrix, she records her question, and tells students that their job is to write three more questions during and after reading that use the "what is" stem to generate questions about the events of the book.

As she continues to read, she pauses to model using the "who is" stem to generate a question in the modified Q-matrix's second column about the characters. She reads, "Their keeper Mr. Gramzay noticed the two penguins" and says, "I wonder more about this character Mr. Gramzay. Who is a keeper? What is his job? Will he be an important person in this book?" After jotting down these questions, she directs the class to think about three more "who" questions for the characters column of the Q-matrix.

The third column of the modified Q-matrix challenges readers to generate four questions about the events of the text, largely beginning with the word "why." When Roy and Silo have an empty nest, they fill it with a rock: "One day Roy found something that looked like what the other penguins were hatching and he brought it to their nest. It was only a rock, but Silo carefully sat on it. And sat . . . and sat." The teacher models a "why" question by asking, "Why would these penguins sit on a rock?" She reminds the class that they are to generate three more "why" questions, based on the book's events.

The final column of the modified Q-matrix challenges the reader to generate a "how" question based on the outcome or results of the events. She seizes on an opportunity when the book reads, "Then Mr. Gramzay got an idea. He found an egg that needed to be cared for, and he brought it to Roy and Silo's nest." She models:

> I wonder where this egg came from. I wonder how it is alone and needing to be cared for. I wonder how Mr. Gramzay came up with this idea. I can turn those

wonderings into questions, and I will write "How did Mr. Gramzay find that egg?" for my first of four questions in this column.

The teacher encourages students to raise a hand throughout the read-aloud to add to the Q-matrix, relying on the question stems and the column headers to scaffold their writing. They also return to the Q-matrix at the conclusion of the book, to pose questions that go beyond the text. Table 5.3 shows the compilation of their work.

As intended by the original Q-matrix, their questions increase in sophistication as children become more adept at the strategy. Their higher-level questions allude to the theme of the book: the diversity of families.

In its original form, the Q-Matrix was intended to assist students in generating questions that advance from least complex to most complex. Its creator envisioned it as a user-friendly way of applying Bloom's Taxonomy. As this teacher provides explicit modeling on the various forms and stems of questions, her students generate both basic and sophisticated questions. With increased practice, they move toward more complex questions: those about present, past, possibility, probability, prediction, and imagination.

Table 5.3 Modified Question Matrix for *And Tango Makes Three*

Event	Person/Characters	Reasons	Results
Complete these questions about the event in the text.	Complete these questions about one or more of the characters.	Complete these questions about the reasons behind the event.	Complete these questions about the results/outcome.
What is a family? What makes a family a family?	Who is a zookeeper?	Why do Roy and Silo sit on a rock?	How did Mr. Gramzay find the egg that became Tango?
What did Roy and Silo do to take care of Tango?	Who did more of the work of taking care of baby Tango?	Why did the zookeeper give Roy and Silo the egg?	How does a chick know when it is time to hatch?
What will happen as Tango grows up?	How would Tango have been different if his egg had gone to another couple?	Why don't more zookeepers give two daddies or two mommies eggs to take care of?	How will Tango be different from the other penguins?
What does a penguin's song sound like?	Who might Mr. Gramzay take care of next?	Why might this family be different than the other zoo families?	How might the story have been different if Roy and Silo had not got this egg?

KWLS

An earlier chapter explored the use of the KWL chart as a tried-but-true question generation strategy. This graphic organizer provides students a forum for the following:

- K (What I Know): Where students activate their background knowledge before reading a text
- W (What I Want to Know): Where students set a purpose for reading—by asking questions or listing what they hope they gain from the text
- L (What I Learned): Where students reflect—after reading—on the knowledge they gained from the text

The following example shows how the KWL chart can be extended into a KWLS chart using an essential question to spark students' questions.

In a classroom in the South Bronx, a teacher opens up a small-group social studies lesson about Gandhi with an essential question. As defined by Wiggins and McTighe (2005), essential questions are juicy questions that stimulate ongoing thinking and inquiry. Essential questions spark discussion and debate, probe into matters of considerable importance, and cannot be answered by a simple "yes" or "no." Essential questions meet the following criteria:

- They are asked and re-asked throughout the unit.
- They demand justification and support.
- Answers may change as understanding deepens.
- They require movement beyond understanding and studying—some kind of action or resolve—pointing toward the settlement of a challenge, the making of a choice, or the forming of a decision.
- They endure, shift and evolve with time and changing conditions.
- They may be unanswerable in the ultimate sense.

To begin her unit on Gandhi, the teacher poses an essential question: "What are the best ways to deal with someone who is treating you unfairly? Is it best to fight or is it best to talk it out peacefully?" This juicy question sparks intense debate among the class, and the teacher uses this essential question as a hook into her lesson on Gandhi. On the classroom computer, she projects two pictures: one of Mahatma Gandhi and the second a map of India. The following conversation unfolds:

> This man was a leader of India, where people who were not white were treated unfairly in the 1940s. He used nonviolence to work peacefully to get fairer

treatment for everyone. Now I'm sure that these pictures and our essential question make you think of some questions that you'd like answered in our reading, so let's use a KWL chart to jot some of those wonderings down.

Students share out the following five questions:

- I want to know why he didn't do violence.
- I want to know how he died.
- Did he have a family?
- Why didn't he want to fight?
- When he was first born, was he treated unfairly like others?

After recording their questions on the whiteboard, the teacher praises their efforts and hands out individual copies of the KWLS chart.

The traditional KWL chart has three columns; this chart divides questions into those generated *before* reading and those generated *after* reading. To highlight the notion that texts do not answer all of students' questions, the chart also includes a fourth column: the S column, to hold the place for questions that students *still* want to address.

Since students are loosely familiar with both Gandhi and the KWL chart, they set to work individually on the K portions of their charts, recording the following background knowledge about Gandhi. The majority of their background information comes from the teacher's quick frontloading instruction, with the essential question and the visual references. Any misinformation in the K column reflects the authenticity of student work.

- He saved India.
- He died.
- He is black.

Table 5.4   KWLS Chart

Before Reading		After Reading	
K	W	L	S
What do I know?	What do I want to know?	What did I learn?	What do I still want to know?

- He is a leader in India.
- Gandhi wanted to help the others in India so it is a better place.
- Gandhi was born in India.
- He didn't want to fight.
- He was treated unfairly.
- He went to school.

After praising them for thinking about what they already knew, the teacher pushes students to generate questions about what they hope the text will answer.

> Next, let's take some time to think of questions that we hope the text will tell us. Some of your questions might piggyback off of what you wrote in the K column. Some might be about the photos I showed you and our essential question. This is the chance to think of as many questions about Gandhi, about India, about nonviolence, and about this time in history as you can.

Students set to work writing their own questions, as the teacher circulates to provide support. For students struggling with the academic language of question generation, she points to the "Wonder Wall," a bulletin board with question starters (e.g., "Who," "What" "How" "When") to jumpstart their thinking.

Table 5.5 lists some of the comprehensive questions generated by individual students.

The nature of these questions reveals the level of each student. For instance, Samantha struggled with the academic language of question generation; to accommodate for her different learning needs, the teacher allowed her questions to be written in the format of "I wonder." Leighton struggled with higher-level thinking and generally generated lower-level questions.

The remainder of the lesson is spent reading a leveled biography of Gandhi. Students are directed to use a sticky note to flag pages that answer the questions in their "What do I want to know?" columns. After reading, they refer directly to the text to share out their findings. They independently record the following new findings in the "What did I learn?" column:

- Gandhi was put in jail.
- He stopped eating.
- He was born on October 2, 1869.
- He went to school in London.
- He took a job in South Africa.
- The unfair people were British.
- Someone in a crowd shot him three times.
- He became a lawyer.

Table 5.5 Before Reading Questions: "What do I want to know?"

Name of Student	Questions Generated
Anya	Was Gandhi the first Indian to make people nice? When was Gandhi born? Where did he go to school?
Fadima	When did he die? When was he born? Did he have a family? Why didn't he fight? Why didn't he do violence? Where was he living?
Samantha	I want to know if Gandhi is old. I want to know if Gandhi wears different clothing. Did he go to school?
Leighton	I want to know if he died. I want to know if he knows karate. I want to know if he's joyful. I want to know if he's relaxed and magical.
Yumaris	How did he die? How did he make India fair? Why didn't he want to fight? Has he ever been to jail?
Oumar	Why is he dead? What did he speak? What was his favorite color? Did he have a family? Did he get married?

With the objective of showing students that one text cannot address all of their questions, the teacher directs students to the column titled, "What do I still want to know?"

Let's look across our W and L columns. We've come a long way in answering some of the questions that you first asked. But some of your questions might linger—that means, you still might want to know their answers. The text might also have made you think of new questions. Good readers know that one book can't answer everything, and good readers are always asking all sorts of questions. So now, let's add to the "What do I still want to know column?" For example, I have a question that this book made me think of. We learned that Gandhi stopped wearing Western clothes and instead wore robes and sandals. I want to know more about this, so I'm going to record this question in my S column: Why did Gandhi only wear sandals and robes? Let's hear some of your S questions.

S1: Why did he fast? What made him think a fast would work?
S2: How long did he stay in jail?
S3: How long can someone fast before dying?

S4: Did Gandhi ever meet Martin Luther King?
S5: Did he have a family? Any kids?
S1: Are things in India fair now?
S3: Why is he bald in all the pictures? Did his hair fall out or did he shave his head?

This teacher has adapted one of the most commonly used reading strategies to place more instructional focus on question generation. As explained in a previous chapter, KWL was originally designed to be a pre-reading activity that encouraged students to activate their background knowledge, to set a purpose for reading, and to monitor their learning from a text. The simple addition of the S column pushes students to generate more questions, either the nagging questions unanswered in the scope of one text or the questions that inevitably arise as learners become more familiar with a topic.

In subsequent lessons, this teacher might bring in supplementary texts that address their unanswered queries or incorporate ways to have students conduct outside research. The power of the "What do I still want to know" column is clear. Not only do the questions in the S column outnumber the questions in the W column, but these fourth-grade students are also better able to address the teacher's initial essential question.

Barell (2008) offers an extension of the KWL chart, as shown below:

K—What do we think we know about the subject?
W—What do we want and need to find out?
H—How will we go about finding answers to our questions?
L—What are we learning as we move along our journey of inquiry and what have we learned at the end of our journey?
A—What action will we take as the result of our inquiry? How can we apply what we have learned?
Q—What new questions do we have as we proceed and after our study of this topic?

CONCLUDING THOUGHTS

In these activities, teachers have modified previously existing question-generation strategies—the Q Matrix and the KWL—to differentiate according to the needs of their students. These activities showcase young students—transitioning from beginning readers to instructional readers—taking ownership for the questions that they generate from poetry, historical fiction, and storybooks. All of these strategies—easily modified according to grade level and for parents at home—showcase how questions increase in breadth and depth as students are increasingly given modeling and practice.

THINK ABOUT IT

- For a few days, keep an "I Wonder" journal. Jot down questions you have about occurrences, observations, and events. What did the experience reveal about yourself as a learner?
- Choose a topic that you know a fair amount about—perhaps a skill like knitting or gardening or a topic you studied. Practice making a KWLS chart about it. How many questions can you generate on the "S" column? What will you do with the "S" column for your future learning?

Chapter 6

Questioning Inside Third-Grade Classrooms

"We get wise by asking questions, and even if these are not answered, we get wise, for a well-packed question carries its answer on its back as a snail carries its shell."

—James Stephens

This chapter follows third graders in the following question-generation strategies: (a) a modified version of Reciprocal Teaching and (b) "Dear Teacher," in which students and teachers generate and respond to questions in ongoing journal entries.

THIRD GRADERS IN CONTEXT

By third grade, students are expected to have basic reading and writing skills and to begin to apply those skills to a variety of academic contexts. Reading researchers often refer to this as the pivotal shift from "learning to read" to "reading to learn" (Chall, Jacobs, and Baldwin, 1990). In previous grades ("learning to read"), the majority of instruction focuses on word study and phonic skills to help students develop the automaticity to decode texts. In third grade and beyond, instruction focuses on acquiring knowledge and content from a variety of texts, or "reading to learn."

Third graders are becoming smoother, more efficient, more fluent readers. As a result of their increasing fluency, third graders tend to read more on their own and to understand more of what they read. In third grade, students develop the following foundational literacy skills:

- Master decoding skills to easily read single syllable words and to analyze/break down unfamiliar words into their parts
- Recognize common word patterns in longer words
- Read approximately 120 words per minute
- Have solid reading comprehension for a variety of text structures
- Pinpoint the main idea and supporting details, distinguish between fact and opinion, and answer factual questions in expository text
- Identify themes, recognize character traits and motivations, and retell narrative stories in sequence

More specifically, the Common Core State Standards hold third graders to the following English Language Arts reading expectations:

- Ask and answer questions to demonstrate understanding of a text, referring explicitly to the text as the basis for the answers
- Recount stories, including fables, folktales, and myths from diverse cultures; determine the central message, lesson, or moral; and explain how it is conveyed through key details in the text
- Describe characters in a story (e.g., their traits, motivations, or feelings) and explain how their actions contribute to the sequence of events
- Determine the meaning of words and phrases as they are used in a text, distinguishing literal from nonliteral language
- Refer to parts of stories, dramas, and poems when writing or speaking about a text, using terms such as *chapter*, *scene*, and *stanza*; describe how each successive part builds on earlier sections
- Distinguish their own point of view from that of the narrator or those of the characters
- Explain how specific aspects of a text's illustrations contribute to what is conveyed by the words in a story (e.g., create mood, emphasize aspects of a character or setting)
- Compare and contrast the themes, settings, and plots of stories written by the same author about the same, or similar, characters (e.g., in books from a series)
- By the end of the year, read and comprehend literature, including stories, dramas, and poetry, at the high end of the grades 2–3 text complexity band independently and proficiently

Reciprocal Teaching

As explained by Palinscar and Brown (1986), Reciprocal Teaching is an instructional activity that incorporates the multiple reading comprehension strategies of summarizing, question generating, clarifying, and predicting.

As the teacher and students take turns at leading this dialogue, the following essential elements are kept in mind:

1. Group students heterogeneously. Stronger readers can support weaker students. Groups of four are ideal.
2. Give students the title of the article or a view of the cover (if there is one). Have students use this to make a prediction about the text they will read. After two to three minutes to write predictions, allow groups to share predictions. The teacher may write these predictions on the board.
3. As they read, students should record in the question box any questions they have or unknown vocabulary words.
4. After everyone has finished reading the article, have groups discuss their questions. Have them help each other clarify these questions. Their answers and clarifications go in the clarify box.
5. After groups finish questioning and clarifying, students independently summarize the article. Example prompts include "I now understand" or "This article explained . . ."

In a second-grade classroom, a teacher is determined to demonstrate that even young readers can tackle the complexities of Reciprocal Teaching. She follows the adaptations provided by Myers (2005) and Strickin (2011) to make this technique approachable for second graders. Strickin proposed introducing Reciprocal Teaching through the use of characters, props, and costumes:

- *Paula the Predictor* wears a scarf and holds a crystal ball to help make predictions about what might happen in a book.
- *Clarence the Clarifier* wears glasses and holds a magnifying glass to help solve the mysteries in a text. He looks for clues in the text to help understand words and ideas.
- *Quinn the Questioner* is a game-show host who holds a toy microphone. He is largely responsible for generating questions within and beyond a text.
- *Sammy the Summarizer* wears a cowboy hat and holds a lasso. He lassos information to determine the main idea of a text.

As Strickin (2011) noted, "elementary students find these characters very entertaining and cannot wait for a chance to 'be' each one" (p. 621).

The teacher pulls a small group of readers and aims to elicit questions using Reciprocal Teaching with the text *Chicken Little*. The folktale tells the story of Chicken Little, who thinks that the sky is falling when she is hit by an acorn. She tells her friends—Henny Penny, Ducky Lucky, and Loosey Goosey. The group runs into Foxy Loxy, who advises them to look up into the sky. His aim is to sneak up and eat them, while they are distracted. When the characters realize Foxy Loxy's ulterior motives, they run away to safety.

As this book is written at their independent reading levels, the students are able to navigate it on their own. The teacher, however, sets them up for success in the question generation, the least familiar of the strategies.

> Our most important character today is going to by Quincy the Questioner. Quincy likes to ask questions about the text—questions that are answered right in the book itself and questions that might not be answered directly in the book. We are going to take turns reading aloud—if you've got a question to ask, I'd like to you raise your hand. When I see your hand, I will pass you Quincy's microphone and you can ask us your question. When you are acting as Quincy, I also want you to explain how you came up with that question. Behind me, you'll see a pocket chart with question stems that might help you think of some of the questions you encounter as you read. Feel free to use those stems to start your questions.

The pocket chart holds the following sentence stems:

- I wonder . . .
- I'd like to know more about . . .
- Why is . . . so important?
- What is your opinion of . . .?
- What is the author's opinion of . . .?
- What is the author trying to make me think, feel, or do?
- Did I learn anything that was new to me?
- How is this like/different from . . .?

She models her efforts to act like Quincy the Questioner. When she reads the line, "The sky is falling. I must tell the king," she picks up the microphone and asks, "Why does Chicken Little want to tell the king? What does she think the king will do?"

Because students are somewhat familiar with Reciprocal Teaching, they are eager to act as Quincy the Questioner. She hands the microphone to one student who explains the origin of her question:

> On this page, I noticed that the illustrator made the words go down the page, instead of across. It sort of looks crooked. I want to ask, "Why did the illustrator draw this word like that?"

Another child refers the group to the line, "Along the way, she met Henny Penny." The child recounts her question: "Will Henny Penny believe Chicken Little about the falling sky? How will Chicken Little feel if Henny Penny does not believe her?" A boy explains his question:

Chicken Little says that she can feel that the sky is falling because a little piece of it fell on her tail. This makes me wonder about chicken's tails. Do chickens use their tails to feel things? Are their tails like our hands?

Several students share out the following questions:

- Why were they all screaming, "Run"?
- Why did Foxy Loxy trick the birds?
- Why did the fox try to eat the birds?
- Why did Chicken Little find her friends?
- Why do the birds' names all sound the same?
- Why does the fox love feathers so much?
- Why are they all birds?

At the conclusion of the text, the students pause to address some of their unanswered questions. They decide that Chicken Little finds her friends because she is scared and does not want to be alone. One child suggests that the birds intend to find the king so that everyone in the kingdom can be safe from the falling sky and stay inside. Another child astutely draws a connection between the fox in this book and the wolf in Little Red Riding Hood. He poses the question, "How are the fox and the wolf alike?"

The majority of questions are not answered in the text. Though the small group of readers can make hunches about the origins of the birds' names and the use of birds as characters, these answers are not explicitly provided. Their questions open up a rich conversation about the author's intentions and choices—perhaps a conversation that may not have occurred without the use of Reciprocal Teaching as a question-generation strategy.

"Dear Teacher"

In a third-grade classroom in Brooklyn, students use their thirty-minute independent reading block to flip through the newspaper. In individual conferences at the beginning of the year, the teacher discovers that none of the students have ever read a daily newspaper. This teacher seizes on an opportunity to allow students to critically engage with a newspaper. He provides his students with individual copies of *The New York Times* and encourages them to independently navigate the text.

Rather than giving his students heavy-handed guidance on how to approach this text, he allows them total freedom to explore the newspaper. To provide them with some structure and direction in this largely unstructured instructional format, he directs students to generate questions:

As you navigate the newspaper, I want you to jot down questions that you have about the paper. The questions can come from pictures you see, headlines that you read, or other portions of the paper that spark questions that pop into your mind. Sometimes there is information overload in a newspaper, so focus on the things that are of particular interest to you. In your journal, I've started a page titled "Dear Teacher." This is your opportunity to write down questions that you'd like me to answer specific to this newspaper. Tomorrow when you come back, I will have written you a letter where I would have done my best to answer these questions.

After thirty minutes of independently navigating through the newspaper, two students submit their questions. In his prep period, the teacher does a side-by-side comparison of both journals and generates a letter to both students. More specifically, he notes the following trends in both sets of questions:

- How do you get a job writing for a newspaper?
- Who is in charge of *The New York Times*?
- How was *The New York Times* created?
- Why is *The New York Times* so important?

Noting the commonalities of questions regarding the structures, organization, titles, and authors of the newspapers, he drafts a response to his students. The overlap in the two sets of questions leads him to write a uniform introductory paragraph for both students. He also discovers that some of their thought-provoking questions force him to do his own outside research. His objective in his "Dear Students" letters is not merely to provide explicit answers to their questions but to use this communication as a means to help build their understanding of navigating the largely unfamiliar text genre of newspapers.

Dear Students,

First off, thank you for your extremely intelligent questions. This was a difficult assignment—and very open-ended. So thank you for taking the time to try to understand an adult newspaper such as the *New York Times* in all of its complexity. Now that you have had the opportunity to look through this amazing newspaper on your own, here are a few things you should understand that might help frame your thinking.

The *New York Times* is organized into sections. These sections include US News, International News, Sports, Film, Art, Books, and Music. Each section includes articles on that subject. In the Sports section you will find articles about sports. In the US News section you will find stories about the United States Government and Culture. In the Film section you will find stories about new films that are coming out in theaters, and, of course, in the Sports section, you will learn all about recent events in major sports like basketball, soccer, baseball, and football.

Unlike the texts that we read, a newspaper is written by many different authors who specialize in writing on a particular subject. The sports writers are usually experts in sports and can provide the reader with the most informed thoughts and opinions. Many readers of the *New York Times* will read the articles in sections that are of interest to them and skip other sections. For example, I always read the sports section and the US News section, but I rarely read the Fashion section.

One of the things that you pulled out from your reading of the newspaper is that the titles of articles are extremely important! This is because there are so many articles that the authors have to summarize the article and catch the interest of the reader. This is called a "headline." A headline is the title of a newspaper article that is written by the author to capture the interest of the reader as he or she is skimming through the newspaper.

I hope you enjoyed getting the chance to skim through an adult newspaper. We can try this again if it is of interest, and feel free to write down any further questions you might have. See my responses below.

Fondly,
Your Teacher

Next, he closely examines the questions from each student and generates a letter for each individual reader. James, an avid athlete, focuses the bulk of his reading on the Sports section. He writes the following response.

Dear James,

I could tell from your letter that you are really interested in sports! I've seen you play basketball on the playground; I wonder if you play on a team outside of school. Since I don't have time to answer all of your questions, I thought I'd focus on the questions you generated about sports.

1. *Why do some sports categories repeat "Baseball, Pro Hockey, Golf, NBA Basketball, Tennis, and Soccer?"*
   The Sports section usually covers the major sports. The purpose of these articles is usually to inform the reader of recent events and news in the sports world. The sports section is usually divided further into sections on each sport, so the basketball articles are all grouped together for the reader, as are the football articles. This allows the reader to navigate to the articles that are of the most interest. I, for example, like to read all of the NBA articles but don't read any of the Football articles. Therefore it is helpful for the NBA articles to be sectioned together and titled "Basketball."
2. *"Providence, the Last Team In, Beats BU for the Title." Did Boston hold the title or does each college or university fight for it?*
   I'm glad you wrote down the title of this article, because the title usually explains a lot about the article. I can tell you that BU is the abbreviation for a college named "Boston University." From the title it looks like BU did not hold the title. They were in the finals, and Providence beat them for the title in the finals.
3. *"Pro Basketball (Section)": Were the Bulls playing the 76ers when Rose left or returned to the Bulls this season?*
   I'm glad you noted the section. The Bulls were playing the 76ers in 2011 when Rose tore apart his knee. They were not playing the 76ers when he returned but rather when he was injured three years ago.
4. *"Where are the teachers of color?" Is this in most schools?*
   This is a great question. Sometimes authors pose a question as the title of the article and go on to answer that question in the text of the article. To answer this question, you would definitely have to read into the descriptive text. It is very likely that the author provided some answers to this question in the descriptive text.

I hope you enjoy reading my answers as much as I enjoyed reading your questions. If you have more questions, use your Dear Teacher journal to write them, and I will continue writing the answers as best as I can.

Yours truly,
Your Teacher

    Juan's questions are more numerous and do not follow as many patterns as those asked by James.

    Throughout the year, the teacher and students continue their "Dear Teacher" logs. These ongoing journals provide a personal forum between

Dear Juan,

I was impressed by how many questions you asked! I can tell from your questions that you really focused on the titles of each article. This was a great reading skill to apply, as the title gives us so much information! Some of your questions were so thoughtful that I needed to look up the answers on the Internet.

1. *"Met's Meija Suspended 80 Games for Banned Drugs": What does the Met's player have to do to get back in the game, and why did the author include this?*
From the article title, it is clear you found this article in the Sports section. When a player is banned for 80 games, there is usually nothing he or she can do to return to playing before his or her suspension is up. As you know, the purpose of the articles in newspapers is to provide the reader with news about recent events. Since the baseball season is just starting, it is likely that the *New York Times* has many articles about baseball to keep the reader up to date.

2. *"The Blessing and the Curse of a Close Second at Augusta" What the author mean by a blessing and a curse?*
I'm glad that you are thinking so deeply about the titles of the newspaper articles. The titles are extremely important for understanding the main idea of each article. A "Blessing and a Curse" is saying that something is both good and bad. For example, having a very strict fourth-grade teacher will be a blessing because you will learn so much, but it might also be a curse because you will have to work extremely hard and push yourself out of your comfort zones. Another example, it might be a curse if the air conditioner in our classroom breaks down, but it might be a blessing because we might get to go outside during choice time. The author likely chose this title to show that something has both good and bad qualities.

3. *Why is the section "Even When Players Miss Free Throws Teammates Give Them a Hand" and what is the perspective of the person who wrote this article?*
This is a great question. It is difficult to determine the author's perspective without knowing what section of the newspaper this article was in. Usually, the perspective of the authors is neutral (not negative or positive). Sometimes authors write articles in newspapers that are called editorials. These are pieces where the author explicitly has a negative or positive opinion and perspective about a topic and tries to persuade the reader.

4. *"Do Assassins Really Change History?"* Why does the author have second guesses on assassins being positive?
   This is a great question. Sometimes authors pose a question as the title of the article and go on to answer that question in the text of the article. To answer this question you would definitely have to read into the descriptive text. It is very likely that the author provided some answers to this question in the descriptive text/argument.
5. *"One Minor Mystery Solved"* Why does the author think it's a minor mystery?"
   I'm glad you are paying close attention to the titles of articles. This is a great example of a title that the author used to capture the attention of the reader. This is called a headline. Because there are so many articles in a newspaper, each author tries to catch the attention of the reader with a catchy headline.
6. *Why is the picture of President Obama important, and how does it relate to the rest of the text?*
   The picture of President Obama was included on the front page of the newspaper. This photograph pictured President Obama and the leader of the country of Cuba. As we have learned in Informational Reading, photographs always reveal big ideas in the articles. This photograph showed President Obama meeting with the leader of Cuba. This was a historic event because the leaders of these two countries have not met in over fifty years.

I hope you enjoy reading my answers as much as I enjoyed reading your questions. If you have more questions, use your Dear Teacher journal to write them, and I will continue writing the answers as best as I can.

Yours truly,
Your Teacher

the teacher and students to delve into questions, to enhance their personal communication, and to validate the questions posed by individual students. This unique experience gives students the autonomy to navigate a text, to tap into their personal interests, and to get an authentic personalized response. Although a time-consuming effort, the "Dear Teacher" journal could easily be scaled back by having students prioritize the questions they truly want answered. A parent might mimic this opportunity through simple lunch box notes; placing a sticky note in a child's backpack or lunch box with a response to a child's questions would be a powerful forum to provide individual feedback to purposeful questions.

CONCLUDING THOUGHTS

This chapter focuses on how to focus Reciprocal Teaching more specifically on question generation, through the use of characters, props, and actions, with young readers. As children master questioning in the Reciprocal Teaching model, they are more likely to both generate and answer the explicit and implicit questions inherent in a text.

The result is a fluid conversation in which students dig deep into a text, search both within and beyond the text for answers to their questions, and eventually lead meaningful conversations with minimal teacher interference. Additionally, the chapter explores giving children the freedom to navigate an unfamiliar text with the purpose of generating questions about its format, layout, purpose, and content. In the ongoing "Dear Teacher" entries, teachers and students communicate in authentic ways to ask and answer questions outside traditional classroom instruction.

THINK ABOUT IT

- Reciprocal Teaching—though highly effective—is not commonplace in classrooms today. Reflect on both why this might be the case and what your reactions to this strategy are. How might you incorporate elements of Reciprocal Teaching at home and at school?
- How might you use letter writing/journal writing as a means to answer questions posed by individual students?

Chapter 7

Questioning Inside Fourth-Grade Classrooms

"What's the most powerful tool for allowing students to name what they don't know? A question. Not one from us to them, but rather, questions students themselves ask."

—Rothstein and Santana, 2012

This chapter follows classroom teachers as they lead students in generating questions in historical fiction and informational text. Highlighted are three question generation activities: (a) *book bits* where students use tidbits of text to generate-questions about a text both before and after reading; (b) *text feature walks* in historical fiction text; and (c) the *parking lot,* an opportunity to address the frequent off-topic questions that emerge extemporaneously from young readers.

FOURTH GRADERS IN CONTEXT

The typical fourth-grader reader is a preteen who decodes multisyllabic words, reads fluently, but may struggle with reading comprehension. The Common Core State Standards hold fourth-graders to the following English Language Arts reading expectations:

- Refer to details and examples in a text when explaining what the text says explicitly and when drawing inferences from the text
- Determine the theme of a story, drama, or poem from details in the text; summarize the text
- Describe in depth a character, setting, or event in a story or drama, drawing on specific details in the text (e.g., a character's thoughts, words, or actions)

- Determine the meaning of words and phrases as they are used in a text, including those that allude to significant characters found in mythology (e.g., Herculean)
- Explain major differences between poems, drama, and prose, and refer to the structural elements of poems (e.g., verse, rhythm, meter) and drama (e.g., casts of characters, settings, descriptions, dialogue, stage directions) when writing or speaking about a text
- Compare and contrast the point of view from which different stories are narrated, including the difference between first- and third-person narrations
- Make connections between the text of a story or drama and a visual or oral presentation of the text, identifying where each version reflects specific descriptions and directions in the text
- Compare and contrast the treatment of similar themes and topics (e.g., opposition of good and evil) and patterns of events (e.g., the quest) in stories, myths, and traditional literature from different cultures
- By the end of the year, read and comprehend literature, including stories, dramas, and poetry, in the grades 4–5 text complexity band proficiently, with scaffolding as needed at the high end of the range

USING BOOK BITS TO GENERATE QUESTIONS

The following observation comes from a fourth-grade classroom in Brooklyn, New York. These fourth-graders have begun a unit on historical fiction, and their teacher has selected the picture book *Mighty Jackie: The Strike-Out Queen* (Moss, 2004). Not only does the book align with the teacher's intentions to use historical fiction but the book's baseball theme also aligns with the March start of baseball's spring training.

Mighty Jackie tells the true story of Jackie Mitchell, a seventeen-year-old woman whose dream was to be a pitcher for Major League Baseball. The book focuses on a 1931 exhibition game between the New York Yankees and the minor league Chattanooga Lookouts. Raised by a father who reassured her that girls could do anything they set their minds to, Jackie practices tirelessly. Unfazed by a crowd snickering at the site of a woman pitching in Major League Baseball, Jackie strikes out baseball legends Babe Ruth and Lou Gehrig.

To begin her read-aloud, the teacher modifies a pre-reading strategy from Yopp and Yopp (2006). In the book bits activity, the teacher shares short phrases from the text with students prior to reading. These phrases are significant to the text; in selecting the book bits, there is a delicate balance between revealing just enough to help students think about the text and revealing too much to limit the scope of their thinking. The book bits strategy supports young readers in several ways: (a) hooking students and piquing their curiosity about the upcoming book; (b) stimulating their background knowledge; (c) helping students generate predictions; and (d) setting a purpose for reading.

Let's take a closer look at how this teacher used this activity to help students generate questions both before and after reading *Mighty Jackie*.

> Today we are trying out a new activity called book bits. I'm going to give each of you an index card. On the index card, you will find a short phrase that has to do with the book we are about to read. I'm not going to tell you the name of the book, and I'm not going to show you the cover of the book. When you get your book bit, I want you to read it silently to yourself—I will circulate and whisper read to you if you need help. Each book bit tells us something about the setting, the characters, or the actions of today's book.

She stops and distributes the following phrases. Each child sees only one book bit, from the following list:

- Mighty Jackie
- April 2, 1931
- the Chattanooga Lookouts
- New York Yankees
- A nothing team
- Babe Ruth, Lou Gehrig, and Tony Lazzeri
- Only seventeen years old
- A mighty good pitcher
- "You throw like a girl!"
- Fingers were callused
- Hooting and jeering
- Strike three!
- A crowd of four thousand had come to see
- The Babe was striking out

She directs students to silently read their book bits and use them to jot down a quick prediction. She guides them with the question, "What does your book bit tell you about the book? What might we be reading about?"

Students get to work writing in their reading journals. The teacher's stopwatch sounds at the end of three minutes, and she gives the next set of directions.

> Now your job is to mingle with three different people to share your book bits. When you find new people, share out just your book bit. You must read it to your classmate, but you may not discuss anything. No conversation other than

reading your cards! When you've found three people and shared their book bits, I will know you are ready when you sit back in your seat.

The teacher calls on a student to reinforce the directions she has just given out. When she's confident that the class understands the task, she tells them that they will have one minute to practice reading their book bit to themselves out loud.

In a subsequent explanation, she notes that "book bits also provide a bit of oral reading practice, so I give them a brief time to practice their fluency. When they meet with their classmates to exchange bits, I want their delivery of the text to be smooth enough so that another student can comprehend what they are saying. This might not be possible if they don't have a quick minute to practice reading their text aloud."

The classroom is full of the sound of young children reading to themselves; the teacher calls them back together and directs them to begin their mingling. Students push their chairs aside and eagerly search out classmates to share book bits. After about four minutes, all students have returned to their seats; the teacher directs them back to their reading journals to add to and revise their initial predictions. She reminds them, "Think about what you might know about the actions, settings, or characters of the book based on the new book bits." After a few more minutes of silent writing, students share out some of their predictions. The classroom consensus is that the story is about a baseball player named Jackie, and perhaps that is Jackie Robinson.

Next she continues by extending the book bits activity to a question-generation opportunity:

> We know that good readers ask questions about the books they are about to read and about the books that they have read. You did not all get the opportunity to see all of the book bits I selected, so I'm going to show you all of them. We will read through them as a class, and after I show you the entire list, I'd like you to write down three questions that you hope the book answers for you. Remember you can use the sentence starters of *who, what, where, when, why,* and *how* to jumpstart your questions.

After displaying all of the book bits on the SMART Board, she models how she turns a book bit into a question.

> I recognize some of these names—I know that Babe Ruth and Lou Gehrig were famous baseball players, but I'm not familiar with the name Tony Lazzeri. So that's a question that I hope the book answers for me. I will write down "Who is Tony Lazzeri?"

As students set to work, their teacher peers over their shoulders and provides feedback like "How could you rewrite that prediction into a question?" After five minutes of writing, she calls on students to share out their questions, and she transcribes them onto a butcher paper hanging in the front of the room. The list below showcases how students translated book bits into pre-reading questions:

- What happened when a character was only seventeen years old?
- Does the story take place in New York City?
- Is a character in the book jealous of someone?
- Who is being teased for "throwing like a girl"?
- Does Babe Ruth's team win?
- Is Babe Ruth's real name Babe?
- What year does the story take place?
- Who is the "nothing team"?
- Is this book fiction or nonfiction?
- Are the characters kids or adults?
- Is the book about one character or is it about a whole team?
- Is this a true story?

She praises the students for their efforts and directs them to keep these questions in the backs of their minds as they listen to her read *Mighty Jackie*. They listen attentively as the true story of Jackie Mitchell unfolds.

At the conclusion of the book, the teacher uses Google Images to pull up a grainy black- and white-photo of the real Jackie Mitchell. She also reads the author's note at the conclusion of the book, which tells the history behind Jackie Mitchell. The note explains that Virne Beatrice "Jackie" Mitchell Gilbert (August 29, 1913 to January 7, 1987) was one of the first female pitchers in professional baseball. A few days after Mitchell struck out Babe Ruth and Lou Gehrig, the baseball commissioner voided her contract and declared women unfit to play baseball as the game was "too strenuous." Annoyed at constantly feeling like a sideshow, she retired in 1937 at the age of twenty-three.

After the author's note, students return to their initial questions to determine which ones were addressed by the book. Their teacher explains, "Sometimes we have more questions after reading a book—things that the book left unanswered or questions outside the scope of the book. For instance, I want to know why the baseball commissioner voided Jackie's contract. So let me turn that into a question that I will write down on another page. Why did the baseball commissioner void her contract?" Students work to jot down at least two questions they would ask beyond the text. These questions are given below:

- How might baseball today be different if women were able to play?
- Have there been any other female competitors in male sports?
- How did Babe Ruth respond later?
- How did Jackie feel when they discontinued her contract?
- Did Jackie regret her decision to quit baseball?
- Why isn't there women's baseball?
- Did Jackie inspire other girls to start playing baseball?
- What did Jackie do after quitting baseball?
- How did the Yankees feel about Jackie after the game?
- Who won the game between the Yankees and Jackie's team?
- What did the newspapers and the press say about Jackie striking out these famous players?

Book bits is an easily adaptable activity to use portions of a text to encourage children to generate questions. Very young children may need illustrations—instead of words—to springboard their questions. At home, a parent might try this out with young children using a popular picture book like *How Rocket Learned to Read* (Hills, 2010).

Before reading the book, a five-year-old child watches as the reader flips through the pictures, which tell the story of a dog named Rocket who befriends a bird who teaches him to read. The first picture shows Rocket happily napping under a tree, followed by another picture of a bird waking up Rocket by standing on his head. A parent might model using the picture to generate the question, "Why does the bird stand on the dog's head? How does the dog feel?"

Below are sample questions generated by an emergent reader:

- Why is the bird reading a book on a tree?
- Why do dogs like sticks in their mouths?
- What makes dogs feel angry?
- Why do leaves fall off trees in the fall?
- Why do dogs dig?
- Do dogs like snow?
- Why do dogs wag their tails?

Book bits shows that powerful questions can come from small tidbits of text; the activity helps children see that questions can be generated both prior to and after reading the book.

APPLYING PICTURE WALKS TO HISTORICAL FICTION

A familiar adage tells us that "a picture is worth a thousand words." A single image can convey complex ideas, an idea easily extended to the illustrations in a text. An earlier chapter explored picture walks with young readers; the focus here is on older readers using picture walks to generate questions in historical fiction.

The teacher selects a historical fiction text, *Night Boat to Freedom* by Margot Raven (2008). This book tells the story of a boy named Christmas John, who helps free slaves by rowing them to the free state of Ohio. His grandmother, Granny Judith, helps him throughout his dangerous journeys. The teacher might begin by showing the cover picture of the book, which depicts an African American boy—wearing a red shirt—standing in front of some trees. In his hand is a boat paddle.

In her small guided reading group, the teacher holds up the cover and directs the students as follows:

> There's so much going on in the cover of this book. Let's take a close look at it and make a list of the things that you observe. I will jot down your observations, and then we will use that list to ask some questions that we hope the book answers for us. So first, tell me what you see in this cover art.

She acts as a scribe while students call out the details in the cover illustration, as listed below:

- A boy
- A boy in a red shirt
- A boy holding a paddle
- A boy with black skin
- The paddles look worn
- The boy looks tired
- There are trees and leaves in the background
- The title is in cursive

After reviewing this list, the teacher guides the students in turning their observations into questions. She models by explaining, "We all noticed that the boy seems to look sad. That makes me think of some questions that I hope the book answers. Why is this boy sad? Is he sad throughout the entire book? Does he become happier by the end of the book?"

She directs students to try to come up with some questions of their own. Three students are able to work independently. The remainder of the group needs support, and she directs them to use the observations as the prompts for their questions. For example, she models how to turn the observation about the trees and forest in the background into the question, "Does this story take place in a jungle?"

After a few minutes of independent work, students eagerly share out the following questions:

- What time period is this?
- Does the boy live on a boat?
- Where does the story take place? Is it a jungle? Does the boy live in a boat?
- Is there any significance in the red shirt?
- Does the boy use the paddles to row himself somewhere? Does he row someone else somewhere?
- Does the boy in the cover have a family?

With these questions fresh in their minds, the group read the book and use sticky notes to mark the pages where their questions are answered.

The notion of picture walks is simple: Pictures can serve as a meaningful springboard for students to ask questions. Though this example came from only one illustration, it would be prudent to continue generating questions with illustrations throughout a text. Subsequently, a teacher might assign specific pages to individual students (or student partnerships) to cover all the illustrations in a more time-efficient manner. To build student motivation, a teacher could allow students to choose whatever illustration they find to be the most provocative and work independently on their own to generate questions.

Similarly, picture walks are easy for parents to try out as they read aloud at home with their young children. Parents should be sure to push children past merely reporting what they see; instead, the objective here is for parents and children to think about questions to explore while reading. The following prompts may be useful to begin the picture walk:

- What is going on here?
- Who is this?
- When is this story taking place?
- What do you think might happen next?
- How do you think the story might end?
- What are you curious to know more about in the story?

The objective here is to push past the mere observations and predictions that a picture walk naturally generates and have readers turn these observations into questions:

THE PARKING LOT: A SPACE FOR UNANSWERED QUESTIONS

"Why do roller coasters make me barf?"
"When you lose weight, where does it go?"

"Can hair really grow as long as Rapunzel's?"

These questions, scribbled in student handwriting on colorful sticky notes, cover an enormous poster, titled "Parking Lot," hanging in a fourth-grade classroom. For this fourth-grade teacher, the parking lot is as an ongoing log of children's unanswered questions. He explains:

> When kids have a question—one I can't answer or one that is off-topic—I tell them to jot it down and put it in the parking lot. When we've got a couple extra minutes of time, I pull things from the parking lot and try to answer them.

The parking lot is the home for questions that a teacher prefers to leave unanswered for the moment. When a student asks a seemingly off-topic question or a question that could not be immediately answered, the teacher acts as a scribe and records it on the parking lot—be it a classroom poster or a section of a whiteboard. Harmin and Toth (2006) explained that the parking lot "reminds us to handle such deferred questions, assures students that their questions will not be forgotten, and, of course, helps us to keep our lessons flowing with active involvement" (p. 219).

With a tone of resignation, the teacher admits that time has prevented him from fully addressing the questions in the parking lot. He admits that "the parking lot is the place where my students' questions have gone to die." As he aims to bring life back to their unanswered questions, he uses an inquiry-based model that is student-centered, collaborative, and motivating for young readers. He creates student-centered small-group sessions, in which students determine the origin of their parking lot inquiries and purposefully use informational text to address their questions. The list below shows the questions that emerge within the first week of creating the parking lot:

- Why do our hands get wrinkled after we take a bath?
- Why can't penguins fly?
- Why are apples different colors?
- Why don't snakes have feet?
- What are our belly buttons for?
- Why do we drink milk from cows?

To begin, the teacher selects a handful of easily answerable parking lot questions. When students come in the next day, they see some of their parking lot questions recorded on sentence strips. The teacher probes for the origin of each question, with prompts such as, "Can you tell me what made you ask this question?" and "Where did you get the idea for this question?"

Students eagerly reveal why they wrote each question; they point to movies, other books, and everyday experiences as the source of inspiration for their questions. One student's question (What do alligators eat?) stems from Mercer Meyer's (1987) *There's an Alligator Under My Bed*, where an illustration depicts a character luring an alligator with a peanut butter sandwich. Another student poses "Can sharks really smell blood?" after watching the film *Finding Nemo*.

Next, the teacher models how to tackle the parking lot question, "Can hippopotamuses swim?" The question originates from the children's picture book *The Circus Ship* by Chris Van Dusen (2009), which shows a shipwrecked hippopotamus swimming to shore. Using a digital document camera to project an informational text, the teacher overviews the headings, tables of contents, maps, graphs, charts, and indexes. Students direct him to turn to two chapters "Staying Cool" and "River Horses." In a "eureka!" moment, the teacher reads aloud a paragraph explaining that though they spend the majority of their lives submerged in water, hippopotamuses cannot swim nor float.

A student offers, "We should create a freeway poster—that's where the answers to our parking lot questions can go!" The teacher fashioned construction paper into a new poster titled "Freeway: Full Speed Ahead" and recorded "Hippos don't swim!" onto a new sticky note.

In their leveled guided reading groups, students are matched to appropriately leveled text to tackle their parking lot questions; a higher-level group tackled a complex text *Grossology* (Branzei, 2002) to answer the question "Why do I burp?" For groups that need additional support, sticky notes direct students to the relevant pages.

In subsequent weeks, the freeway poster fills up with students' findings. They share out their new knowledge: that sharks can smell blood up to three miles away, that the brown spots on bananas come from the fruit's starches turning into sugar, and that bubbles are round because air pushes evenly in every direction. Students become walking encyclopedias of newfound knowledge: Lobsters' teeth are found in their stomachs, and human beings are taller in space without the pull of gravity.

The parking lot quickly becomes the hottest location in this classroom. Instead of emptying of questions, the sticky notes in the parking lot increase in number. As students see authentic purposes for their questions in informational text, they actively generate questions. Not only do students' questions increase in number, but they also increase in quality. Initially students pose literal and basic questions (e.g., "What do hippopotamuses eat?"). Subsequently, students pose questions that are more analytical, evaluative, and interpretive (e.g., "Where did the myth that elephants are afraid of mice come from?").

The parking lot is appropriate for all levels of readers. If students are not able to write their own questions, the teacher can act as a scribe. In addition to keeping a whole-class parking lot, it may be prudent to encourage students to keep an individual parking lot. Students might jot their own questions in a reading journal, as a way to encourage less vocal students to have a space for their own wonderings.

Teachers can also use the parking lot as a meaningful home-school activity. Teachers might invite parents/caregivers to share the questions that arise at home through email, notes, and photos.

The parking lot is also a popular home activity. A parent might convert an empty space on a closet door or the refrigerator to a parking lot. When a child asks a question, the parent might jot it down on a sticky note and place it on the door. These questions can serve as a conversation starter prior to routine trips to the public library. The parking lot questions help a child and parent to set a purpose for a library trip and to help guide text selection.

Parents might inquire about which questions their child would really like to answer; the child then brings those sticky notes to the library and seeks out texts that might provide reasonable answers to his or her questions. When a young reader asks, "Will my hair grow as long as Rapunzel's?" the parent might help to search out an answer in the ever-popular *Guinness Book of World Records*.

The child is purposeful on the library trip and feels satisfied in discovering that the longest hair on record grew to eighteen feet. Because questions arise at all times of the day (particularly in the car!), parents should keep a pack of sticky notes in their purses and jot them down when afforded the opportunity. This practice encourages children to generate their own questions as they encounter a purposeful trip to the library and meaningful text selection.

CONCLUDING THOUGHTS

The first two activities showcase meaningful ways to have students generate questions prior to reading. With careful modeling and support from teachers, students can generate questions from short portions of text: from a phrase as in book bits and a cover illustration as in a picture walk. As so many of the questions that our children ask don't come in relation to a text, the parking lot reminds parents and teachers that those questions must be addressed later and not go ignored.

THINK ABOUT IT

- Keep a list of student-generated questions in your own parking lot. How do you approach them? How are these questions answered? What incentives do students have to generate more questions?
- What do you do with the questions that stump you? How do you attempt to answer the questions that you cannot or will not address?

Chapter 8

Questioning Inside Fifth-Grade Classrooms

"We get wise by asking questions, and even if these are not answered, we get wise, for a well-packed question carries its answer on its back as a snail carries its shell."

—James Stephens

Thus far, this book has presented question-generation strategies from text illustrations, visual images, and short bits of text. To extend these ideas, this chapter focuses on generating questions from concrete objects, an idea called *An Object a Day*. Also presented is the complex strategy of *Question-Answer Relationship*, covered in detail in chapter 2. Both these strategies present classroom vignettes showcasing juicy questions posed in the independent reading skills of fifth graders.

FIFTH GRADERS IN CONTEXT

As fifth graders approach the "tween" years (between childhood and adolescence), they are asked to read a lot in a variety of subject areas. Their reading of narrative text focuses on character analysis, understanding an author's style and purpose, and recognizing a text's organizational structures. Their writing becomes increasingly complex as they produce and present research projects, and write more complex narratives and creative fiction. As in reading, they explore writing for personal expression.

The Common Core standards hold fifth graders responsible for the following English Language Arts reading expectations:

- Quote accurately from a text when explaining what the text says explicitly and when drawing inferences from the text
- Determine the theme of a story, drama, or poem from details in the text, including how characters in a story or drama respond to challenges or how the speaker in a poem reflects upon a topic; summarize the text
- Compare and contrast two or more characters, settings, or events in a story or drama, drawing on specific details in the text (e.g., how characters interact)
- Determine the meaning of words and phrases as they are used in a text, including figurative language such as metaphors and similes
- Explain how a series of chapters, scenes, or stanzas fits together to provide the overall structure of a particular story, drama, or poem
- Describe how a narrator's or speaker's point of view influences how events are described
- Analyze how visual and multimedia elements contribute to the meaning, tone, or beauty of a text (e.g., graphic novel, multimedia presentation of fiction, folktale, myth, poem)
- Compare and contrast stories in the same genre (e.g., mysteries and adventure stories) on their approaches to similar themes and topics
- By the end of the year, read and comprehend literature, including stories, dramas, and poetry, at the high end of the grades 4–5 text complexity band independently and proficiently

AN OBJECT A WEEK

A staple of early childhood classrooms is show-and-tell time—an opportunity for young children to showcase an object from home and describe it to their peers. There are many academic and social benefits of show-and-tell time, including fostering the home-school connection, fostering oral language skills, refining public speaking, and building children's confidence. The academically rigorous day of upper-elementary grades leaves little room for such practice with older children. In his 2008 book about teaching for inquiry, Barell lamented about the loss of show-and-tell time in classrooms:

> To what extent could we use [show and tell] presentations as opportunities to invite students' curiosities about these objects? Instead of telling us all about their new objects, could students show them and then ask their classmates to observe, think, and ask questions about them? What would be the benefit? (p. 37)

The strategy is modified from Yopp and Yopp's (2006) "Concrete Experiences," where a teacher selects three to five concrete objects that relate to a text. Before reading, the teacher places these small objects in a box and then reveals them one by one to have readers make predictions about how the objects relate to the text. These concrete experiences have many benefits: activating background knowledge and building intrinsic motivation (Guthrie and Ozgungor, 2002) and supporting English learners through meaning making with tangible objects (Peregoy and Boyle, 2009). Of particular relevance to this book, Yopp and Yopp wrote (2013), "A second cognitive benefit of concrete experiences is that they prompt students to ask questions" (p. 44).

These objects challenge students to activate their background knowledge, generate vocabulary, and make inferences about the events or theme of a book prior to reading. Prior to reading *Charlie and the Chocolate Factory*, a teacher might place a chocolate bar, a ticket, and a top hat in a box and ask the readers to predict how each object relates to the book.

Afraid that her fifth graders will find the term "show and tell" too babyish, a teacher incorporates an "An Object a Week" into his routine classroom instruction. Usually integrated into his science instruction, the teacher shares everyday objects with his students that spark their curiosities, evoke their wonderings, and help them generate questions. He has shared seashells, volcanic rocks, seed pods from trees, and bits of coral.

The following vignette comes from a Manhattan classroom, where a teacher brings in a half of a robin's egg that he has discovered in the school courtyard. His discovery is opportune, as his students are just about to begin a thematic unit on the adaptations of living things. He fashions a cushioned shadow box for the egg and brings it in for the next day.

To pique students' curiosity, he holds up the box and explains as follows:

> I've got a mystery object in this box. Today, when it is center time, you will find this object at the Independent Writing center. I will leave some magnifying glasses there as well. Your job is to take a very close look at this mystery object and to write questions that you have about it in your journals. Your questions can be wonderings, like "I wonder if . . ." or "I'd like to know. . . ." Or, you can use the sentence starters of who, what, where, when, why, and how to jump-start your thinking in writing some juicy questions. We will use the questions you ask to begin our science and literacy unit about adaptations.

At their allotted writing center time, students eagerly examine the object and generate lists of questions. Once all students have rotated through the center, the teacher leads a whole-class conversation about the mystery object. Realizing that all of the students understand that the object came from a bird, he asks them to share out some of their questions. Rather than a chaotic session of unstructured questions, it turns out to be a purposeful activity, with the teacher leading them in organizing their questions according to

106   Chapter 8

their structure. When he probes for student-generated wonderings using the "I wonder" and "I'd like to know" prompts, students share out the following:

I wonder . . .

- If this was the only egg from the nest?
- If the baby lived?
- If birds have belly buttons? I wonder if birds have ears?

I'd like to know . . .

- What kind of bird made this?
- If birds have feathers when they are born?

He then leads the students in sharing out questions according to their question stems. As students share out their questions, they piggyback on additional questions from those posed by their peers. When one student alludes to a question about bird migration, several students build off that question—though these were not questions originally posed in their journal writing.

Who?

- Whose egg is this?
- Who came out of this egg?
- Who is the mom of this egg? Who is the dad?

What?

- What kind of bird made this egg?
- What is an egg made of?
- What did birds evolve from?
- What happens when a baby doesn't learn to fly?
- What makes the egg such a bright blue color?
- What are birds' predators?
- What do birds eat?
- What does a baby bird look like?

Where?

- Where is this baby now?
- Where would a baby bird go if it fell out of its nest?
- Where do birds nest?
- Where do they sleep when they fly over big oceans?

When?

- When dinosaurs and birds lived together, did they get along? Or were they enemies?
- When they sit on electric wires, why don't birds get a shock?

Why?

- Why is this egg cracked? Did it fall out of the nest?
- Why don't all birds fly? Why can't a penguin fly? Why can't an ostrich fly?
- Why are birds colorful?
- Why do birds peck on telephone poles?
- Why do birds peck on glass windows and doors?

How?

- How can you tell the male and female birds apart?
- How do birds fly such long distances in the fall?
- How do birds know which direction to fly?
- How does the bird know how to get out of the egg?
- How did the bird get out of the egg?
- How does a bird lay an egg?
- How do birds fly?
- How do birds sing?
- How do baby birds learn to sing? Does their mom teach them?
- How fast do birds fly?
- How do babies catch their food?
- How long does a baby bird live with its mother?

With the simple move of bringing in this concrete object, this teacher has piqued his students' curiosity and motivation to learn about their upcoming thematic unit. His instructional opportunities abound; they will be able to address these questions with informational texts, visits to a neighborhood nature center, websites, and nature magazines written specifically for children. They read *City Hawk: The Story of Pale Male* (McCarthy, 2007), which tells of the red-shoulder hawks living on Fifth Avenue skyscrapers in New York City.

Eventually they participate in a Skype video call with one of the student's grandmothers, who is an avid bird enthusiast. Most certainly, their motivation to undertake this unit of study has been amplified by the questions generated from the object. Barrell (2008) further explained the power of concrete objects to generate questions:

If we want our students to become good observers, sharing their wonderings about objects and experiences with each other and, if appropriate, proceed to search out answers to some of their questions, then we need to help them feel comfortable doing this. We need to model our inquisitiveness; we need to bring in objects to wonder about. (p. 38)

QUESTION-ANSWER RELATIONSHIP

Perhaps the most researched question generation strategy is Question-Answer Relationship (QAR), as explored in depth in chapter 2. The QAR strategy pushes students to formulate an understanding of the variety of questions that are possible for any given passage.

The following vignette comes from a charter school classroom in Brooklyn, New York. This K–5 charter services 650 students, 90 percent of whom qualify for free or reduced lunch. Approximately one of eight students either receives special education services or classifies as an English as a Second Language (ESL) student.

This school uses a scripted curriculum for its English Language Arts instruction and places an enormous emphasis on student performance on standardized tests. In its shared-text approach to literacy across the curriculum, children read about a certain topic in their literature circles and then read another text on the same topic during their social studies instruction. In this fifth-grade classroom, students have covered units on fables, ancient myths, African kingdoms, and world religions.

The teacher has selected a text titled "The First Pilgrims," a brief passage discussing the *Mayflower*, the Pilgrims' first winter in the Americas, and Squanto's actions in keeping them alive. Because his students are largely unfamiliar with the QAR strategy, he uses this text to introduce the four types of questions. His students, however, are well versed in the differences between explicit questions and inferential questions, so he sees QAR as merely introducing new labels to already familiar ideas. He uses the Gradual Release of Responsibility (see Introduction) as the framework to introduce QAR to his students.

In his modeling, he explains the two major categories of questions: In the Book and In My Head. Because his focus is on having students recognize the type of question, rather than the correct answer to the question, he presents them with a list of questions that he has written and leads them in identifying the types of questions.

He models why the question, "Why did the English separate from the Puritans?" is a Right There question because of its answer being explicitly found in the text. He explains the following:

The answer is in the text. The words used to make up the question and words used to answer the question are found in the same sentence. You've sometimes heard me call these "literal questions" because the correct answer can be found somewhere in the passage.

Once clear on the Right There questions, his students are ready to tackle how Think and Search require the reader to search for explicit information in two different sources. He explains the following:

The answer is in the selection, but you need to put together different pieces of information to find it. The answer comes from different places in the selection. You will need to look back at the passage, find the information that the question refers to, and then think about how the information or ideas fit together.

He talks students through question, "Who created Thanksgiving and when?" emphasizing how the answers are both explicit and located in more than one location.

After additional discussion about Right There and Think and Search, students demonstrate their understanding of explicit text-based questions. The teacher reminds them that *In My Head* questions address the questions that go beyond the text. More specifically, he differentiates between the two types: Author and You and On My Own.

Both types of In My Head questions don't have answers in the story. For Author and You, the reader acts like a detective to add together what you already know with what the author tells you to determine how it fits together. These questions require you to use ideas and information not stated directly in the passage to answer. So you must think about what you have read and formulate your own ideas or opinions. For On My Own, the reader can answer the question without even reading the text. The answer is based solely on your own experiences and knowledge. The question is related to the theme or the idea of a text, but does not require anything directly from the text for its answer. A good On My Own question might be, "How does your family celebrate Thanksgiving?" We can all answer that—regardless of whether we have read this text.

After discussing the four different types of questions, the teacher presents the class with a list of questions he has generated and challenges them to work collaboratively to sort the questions according to type. Again, he is not interested in their ability to answer the questions correctly, but rather he wants to assess their ability to understand the question classification system of QAR. After ten minutes, the class classifies the QARs as displayed in table 8.1.

He is confident that as students correctly identify the type of question, they will build their accuracy in seeking out the correct answers.

Sensing that students are ready for collaborative and independent practice, he begins the next day of instruction with a text about Medusa and the Greek goddess Athena. The text tells of Medusa, who constantly boasts of her beauty. One day, Medusa and her friends went to visit the Parthenon, the biggest temple in Greece. While visiting the temple, Medusa compared her beauty to that of the gods and, in particular, declared herself more beautiful than Athena, the revered goddess of beauty and wisdom.

Offended by her egoism, Athena punished Medusa by turning her into a terrible monster. Her hair was made of hissing snakes, and her body was transformed into a snake. As a final insult, Athena told Medusa that anyone who would look into her eyes would be irreparably turned into stone.

After reading the story, the teacher distributes a two-sided graphic organizer. On the front of the organizer, students are given four questions related to the story of Medusa. He gives students five minutes to read each question and label each with the appropriate type of QAR. The questions are as follows:

1. What was the name of the Greek goddess of beauty and wisdom? *Right There*
2. Why was Athena upset with Medusa, and what did Athena do as a result? *Think and Search*
3. Do you agree with Athena's action of turning Medusa into a snake? *Author and Me*
4. What do you think it means to be beautiful? *On My Own*

Table 8.1 List of QAR Questions from *The First Pilgrims*

In the Book	
Right There	Think and Search
• What kind of group were the Pilgrims? • What did the Puritans want to separate from? • What caused Thanksgiving? • How long did the *Mayflower's* journey take?	• Who created Thanksgiving and when? • When was Squanto kidnapped and why? • What did Squanto do to help and what was the result? • Explain what made the Pilgrims' first winter in America so difficult.
In My Head	
Author and You	On My Own
• Why do you think Squanto was kidnapped? • Was it a good or bad thing that Thanksgiving was created? • Would you help the Pilgrims like Squanto did?	• Why is Thanksgiving an important holiday? • How did your family arrive in America? • What makes moving to a new place difficult?

The students then come together to share out their answers and defend their choices. The group correctly identifies the first two questions as In The Book, as the answers are explicitly stated in the text. They understand that the second question requires multiple sources of information, and is thus a Think and Search.

Discussion ensues about the In My Head questions; when students understand that their opinions about beauty can be addressed without actually reading the text, they see the classification of On My Own.

The teacher then leads them in searching out the answers to these questions. He directs, "Now that you've done the hard work of knowing what type of question this is, it will be easier to find the correct answers to these questions." Students are successful in their search for answers. He has them point directly to the portion of the text that addresses the In The Book elements. He challenges them to explain their opinions of beauty with open-ended prompts such as, "Can you say more about that?" and "Tell me why you feel that way."

With the evidence that students can recognize and address the different QARs, he shifts the responsibility to the students to generate their own questions. Knowing that explicit questions are generally easier to generate, he provides students with the following In the Book question stems:

Right There

- What did . . .
- Who did . . .
- How many . . .
- What was . . .
- Who are . . .
- When did . . .
- What does . . .
- What kind . . .
- Who is . . .
- What is . . .
- Where is . . .
- Name . . .
- List . . .

Think and Search

- How do you . . .
- What happened to . . .
- How long did . . .
- What time did . . .
- What happened before . . .

- How would you describe . . .
- What examples . . .
- Where did . . .
- How do you make . . .
- Why does . . .
- Explain . . .
- Compare . . .

Students first work with a partner in a collaborative learning opportunity to generate In the Book questions. They then work independently to generate additional questions. The teacher acts as a scribe, jotting down their In the Book questions.

With this comprehensive list, he directs students to "turn and trade." They jot down their three juiciest questions, careful not to label them with the appropriate type of query. In an engaging forum, they take their questions and mingle with their classmates as if they are at a "grown-ups' cocktail party." He sets a timer, tells students to push in their chairs, and directs them to share out their three questions with a classmate. In this mock cocktail party, students challenge one another to identify the type of questions they have generated. Though the classroom is a bit noisy, all students are engaged as they mingle and attempt to stump each other with their queries.

Next, he leads the students in generating the implicit questions in the In My Head category, using the following prompts:

Author & Me

- Do you agree with . . .

Table 8.2 In the Book Questions from "Medusa and the Greek Goddess Athena"

Right There	Think and Search
• What did Medusa do at the Parthenon? • Who did Medusa offend? • What kind of god was Athena? • Where does this story take place? • Where was the Parthenon? • What did Medusa's friends do? • What did Athena do to punish Medusa? • What happens when people look into Medusa's eyes? • What was Medusa turned into?	• Who did Medusa boast to about her beauty? • What happened to Medusa at the end of the story? • What happened before Medusa went to the Parthenon? • What happened after Medusa offended Athena? • What examples are there of Medusa being vain? • Explain how Medusa boasted about her beauty. • How would you describe Medusa at the beginning of the story?

- Why did the main character . . .
- What did they mean by . . .
- How did she/he feel when . . .
- Give reasons why . . .
- What do you think . . .
- What if . . .
- What do you think will happen . . .
- What did the author mean by . . .
- What did the character learn about . . .

On My Own

- Have you ever . . .
- What are the reasons that . . .
- If you could . . .
- If you were going to . . .
- What are the pros and cons of . . .
- Do you know anyone who . . .
- How do you feel about . . .
- What is your favorite . . . why . . .
- What do you do when . . .
- What can be exciting about . . .
- What do you already know about . . .
- What would you do if . . .

Table 8.3 provides a comprehensive list of the implicit student-generated questions.

Table 8.3 In my Head Questions from "Medusa and the Greek Goddess Athena"

Author & Me	On My Own
• Do you agree with how Athena punished Medusa?	• In your opinion, what is beauty? What does it mean to be beautiful?
• Why did Medusa see herself as better than everyone?	• Is it important to be beautiful?
• How do you think Medusa will feel about her appearance?	• What would you do if someone insulted your appearance?
• What did Medusa learn about vanity and arrogance?	• If you could punish someone for boasting or bragging, how would you punish them?
• Give the reasons why Medusa is considered arrogant.	• How do you feel about vanity and arrogance?
• What if Medusa had not insulted Athena?	• Do you know anyone who is vain or arrogant?
• Was Athena justified in giving such a harsh punishment?	

As they share out their questions, a conversation naturally follows. Students eagerly debate the pros and cons of the punishment given by Athena. They evaluate Medusa's arrogance and vanity and conclude with a conversation about the true meaning of beauty. Not only have these students mastered the QAR format, but they are also able to use the question-generation strategy to engage in rich conversations about the theme of this text.

CONCLUDING THOUGHTS

At the end of their elementary school careers, fifth graders certainly have the language and cognitive skills to generate questions. As the narrowed curriculum and test preparation leave little room for students' natural curiosity, teachers must rise to the challenge of finding innovative, time-efficient means to pursue student questioning. Through concrete objects, students have the ability to generate questions in a cross-curricular format. QAR drives student readiness for multiple choice questions and student-generated questions with true "staying power" (Raphael and Au, 2005, p. 221).

THINK ABOUT IT

- Select a concrete object that you might share with colleagues or friends. What would that object be? What questions might people naturally ask about this object?
- In a day and age where high-stakes testing is pervasive, how might QAR help prepare students for these tests?

Afterword

"Isn't this one of the roles of education—equipping children to ask and answer their own questions, giving them the skills and tools to continue asking and answering the questions that frame our lives?"

—(Julianne Wurm, 2005, p. 84)

Writing this book opened my eyes to the role of juicy questions in my life: my life as a student, as a parent, and as an educational researcher. Though I don't recall being a particularly inquisitive student in grade school, this changed as I entered the field of education. My motivation to become a teacher stemmed largely from my questions about the educational inequity between low-income students and their wealthier peers. As a doctoral student, I asked juicy questions about teachers' instructional decisions and practices in teaching reading comprehension; these questions led to my dissertation and subsequent research agenda. In my work as a reading clinician providing remedial instruction to struggling readers, I noticed an important trend: I was quick to ask low-level questions to assess my students' comprehension, but I provided few opportunities for students to generate these questions themselves. Moreover, my questions did little to provide models for, and scaffold, my students in generating juicy questions themselves.

In summer 2014, I attended a literacy retreat spearheaded by literacy guru Kylene Beers. She recounted a powerful story that she had witnessed in a third-grade classroom. During a unit on ocean life, the students learned that the salinity levels of ocean water are nearly identical to the salinity levels of the human body's blood, sweat, and tears.

Dr. Beers told of a student who raised his hand, with a puzzled look on his face, and posed the following juicy question:

"So if our body has the same amount of salt as the ocean, why do my eyes sting when I open them while swimming in the ocean?[1]" Dr. Beers let this question sink in, as the room full of teachers mulled over a possible answer to this juicy question. As I listened to this vignette, I thought about my own road in question generation as a teacher and as educational researcher. The seed for this book was planted.

Not only am I immersed in questions as a former classroom teacher and current teacher educator/educational researcher, but juicy questions surround me at home—as I explained in the preface. In my daughter's pre-kindergarten class, an entire unit of study emerged from one simple question: "Why are castles special?" This question stemmed from the children's natural curiosities.

For several weeks, the teachers observed the children using the classroom blocks to build castles. Perhaps inspired by the recent release of the movie *Frozen*, the girls spent their free play time building castles for Anna and Elsa—the film's feature characters. Boys engaged in parallel play and built castles for knights and dragons. As the teachers explained:

> A few girls used dolls and figurines each day to build elaborate houses and castles. They invented elaborate scenarios and stories and imagined a world of queens and princesses. Soon the rest of the class joined in, and a parent came in to read aloud Tommie dePaulo's *The Knight and the Dragon*. Some of the children shared their background knowledge about castles and knights—perhaps influenced by a popular Nick Jr television series, *Mike the Knight*.

Underpinning these teachers' instructional approach was the Reggio theory of early childhood education, in which teachers "allow the children's questions and wonderings to guide the curriculum" (Dutton, 2012, p. 4). The Reggio approach uses children's questions as the starting point for thematic instruction.

To ensure that their interest was genuine and not fleeting, the teachers observed children during independent play over the course of a few weeks. As they returned time and time again to conversations around castles, the teachers added books to the classroom library about castles, medieval times, dragons, and knights. During a read-aloud, a particularly inquisitive child posed the juicy question, "What makes a castle a castle?" As children eagerly shared out their ideas, the teachers realized that their natural wonderings were a logical starting point for a unit of instruction centered around medieval times.

Over the course of three months, the class engaged in a multidisciplinary, child-centered thematic unit. One book led to the discovery that kings had

---

[1] In actuality, the percentage of salt in the human body is about 0.9 percent by weight. In seawater, however, it is, on average, around 3.5 percent (35 g/L). Therefore, the concentration is generally higher in seawater.

treasure chests and wore medallion necklaces. The class then began an art project where they designed medallion necklaces and treasure chests full of sixpence. As a math extension, they counted sixpence and learned about money systems.

Using sugar cubes, they constructed a working castle, complete with a drawbridge and a moat. They built a pulley and practiced transporting items up and down from the classroom's loft. A music extension included singing "Sing a Song of Sixpence." They baked bread and ate it with honey. The local nature center brought in a "dragon" (a bearded dragon lizard). The children painted their own coat of arms, a way for knights to identify their families. They designed crowns and medieval hats, all of which were worn at a culminating feast.

An essential element of this lesson was reading and writing integration. The children drew and wrote about castles in their journals. They acquired new vocabulary words. During free play on the playground, the children acted out the roles of people within the castle. The bridge on the playground became the drawbridge to the castle. They built moats and castles in the sandbox. Over the course of three months, this classroom exemplified how a few good questions are enough to propel students' learning in a naturalistic and motivating forward direction.

In a conversation I had with my former doctoral student and a veteran first-grade teacher, he reported the following:

> As an educator, I see that somehow the questions begin to fade away in the confines of a structured educational environment. I believe young children are taught not to ask these free-flowing questions and encouraged instead to focus on a predetermined curriculum. If the curriculum does not interest the student, he becomes complacent. Natural curiosity takes on limitations. Educators want children to focus, but I find that they already are focused—just not always on what I would like.

As evidenced in this preschool classroom and the vignettes in this book, the process of generating juicy questions has a snowball effect. As children become more proficient in generating questions, they eagerly ask more. Barrell (2008) explained that "questioning improves as we learn more. The more information we gather, and the more opportunities we have to ask questions about new learning, the better our questions can become" (p. 190).

My purpose in this book is to highlight not only the importance of addressing students' questions but also the need for teachers and parents to *teach* children how to ask juicy questions. Chouinard and her colleagues (2007) called children's questions "a mechanism for cognitive development." They wrote:

The ability to ask questions to gather needed information constitutes an efficient mechanism for cognitive development . . . the ability to ask questions is a powerful tool that allows children to gather information they need in order to learn about the world and solve problems in it.

These same researchers outline a question-generation cognitive development plan hinging on five essential elements:

1. Children must actually ask questions that gather information.
2. Children must receive informative answers to their questions if they are to be of use to cognitive development.
3. Children must be motivated to get the information they request, rather than asking questions for other reasons, such as seeking attention.
4. The questions that children ask must be relevant and of potential use to their cognitive development.
5. Parents and teachers must see evidence that children's questions help them in some way—that they can ask questions for a purpose and use the information they receive to achieve some change in their knowledge state.

The examples in this book show that powerful transformations happen when we shift from having kids *answer* questions to having kids *ask* questions. When teachers tap into the natural curiosity of children, students are motivated to answer their questions in a variety of authentic texts. The role of the teacher should be to initiate, facilitate, and guide the inquiry process. Teachers and parents must carve time and space in homes, classrooms, and libraries for the questions that young children naturally pose.

The opportunities for juicy questions are limitless. Visualize classrooms where children use bits from text, visual images, graphic organizers, concrete objects, and journals to brainstorm juicy questions. Imagine homes where parents sit around the dinner table and probe their children with, "Did you ask a good question today?" When it comes to promoting cognitive development, motivating students, and creating engaging inquiry-based classrooms, the question is the answer.

References

Allington, R. (2014). Reading moves: What not to do. *Educational Leadership, 72*(2), 16–21.

Allington, R. L. and Weber, R. M. (1993). Questioning questions in teaching and learning from texts. In B. Britton, A. Woodward and M. Binkley (Eds.), *Learning from textbooks: Theory and practice* (pp. 47–68). Hillsdale, NJ: Erlbaum.

Barell, J. (2008). *Why are school buses yellow? Teaching for inquiry preK–5.* Thousand Oaks, CA: Corwin Press.

Beers, K. (2003). *When kids can't read: What teachers can do.* Portsmouth, NH: Heinemann.

Berger, W. (2014). Chasing beautiful questions. *Spirit.* 68–75.

Blackwell, B. (2005). *Classroom motivation from A to Z: How to engage your students in learning.* New York: Routledge.

Bloom, B. (1956). *Taxonomy of educational objectives: The classification of educational goals, handbook I: Cognitive domain.* New York: Longman Green.

Cazden, C. (2001). *Classroom discourse: The language of teaching and learning.* Portsmouth, NH: Heinemann.

Chall, J. S., Jacobs, V. A., and Baldwin, L. E. (1990). *The reading crisis: Why poor children fall behind.* Cambridge, MA: Harvard University Press.

Chien, C. (2013). Using Raphael's QARs as differentiated instruction with picture books. *English Teaching Forum, 3,* 20–25.

Chin, C., Brown, D., and Bruce, B. (2002). Student-generated questions: A meaningful aspect of learning in science. *International Journal of Science Education, 24,* 521–49.

Chouniard, M. M., Harris, P. L., and Maratsos, M. P. (2007). Children's questions: A mechanism for cognitive development. *Monographs of the Society for Research in Child Development, 72*(1), 1–129.

Ciardiello, A. V. (2012/2013). Did you ask a good common core question today? The cognitive and metacognitive dimensions of enhanced inquiry skills. *Reading Today, 30*(3), 14–16.

Cohen R. (1983). Self-generated questions as an aid to reading comprehension. *The Reading Teacher, 36*, 770–75.

Coley, J. D., DePinto, T., Craig, S. and Gardner, R. (1993). From college to classroom: Three teachers' accounts of their adaptations of reciprocal teaching. *The Elementary School Journal, 94*, 255–66.

Common Core State Standards Initiative. (2010). *Common core stand standards for English language arts and literacy in history/social studies, science, and technical subjects.* Retrieved from http://corestandards.org/assets/CCSSI_ELA%20Standards.pdf.

Cortese, E. (2003). The application of Question-Answer Relationship strategies to pictures. *The Reading Teacher, 57*(4), 374–80.

Danielson, C. (2013). The framework for teaching evaluation instrument, 2013 edition: The newest rubric enhancing the links to the Common Core State Standards, with clarity of language for ease of use and scoring. ISBN: 978-0615597829.

Davey, B. and McBride, S. (1986). Effects of question-generation training on reading comprehension. *Journal of Educational Psychology, 78*, 256–62.

Dewitz, P., Jones, J., and Leahy, S. (2009). Comprehension strategy instruction in core reading programs. *Reading Research Quarterly, 44*(2), 102–26.

Doolittle, P. E., Hicks, D., Triplett, C. F., Nichols, W. D., and Young, C. A. (2006). Reciprocal teaching for reading comprehension in higher education: A strategy for fostering the deeper understanding of texts. *International Journal of Teaching and Learning in Higher Education, 17*(2), 106–18.

Dreher, M. J. and Gambrell, L. B. (1985). Teaching children to use a self-questioning strategy for studying expository prose. *Reading Improvement, 22*, 2–7.

Duke, N. (2000). 3.6 minutes per day: The scarcity of informational texts in first grade. *Reading Research Quarterly, 35*(2), 202–24.

Duke, N. (2004). The case for informational text. *Educational Leadership, 61*(6), 40–44.

Durkin, D. (1993). Teaching them to read (6th ed.). Boston, MA: Allyn & Bacon.

Dutton, A. S. Retrieved from https://www.naeyc.org/files/naeyc/file/vop/Dutton_0512_Final1.pdf

Ezell, H. K., Kohler, F. W., Jarzynka, M., and Strain, P. S. (1992). Use of peer-assisted procedures to teach QAR reading comprehension strategies to third-grade children. *Education and Treatment of Children, 15*(3), 205–27.

Fisher, D., Frey, N., and Williams, D. (2002). Seven literacy strategies that work. *Reading and Writing in the Content Areas, 60*(3), 70–73.

Fletcher, J., Simos, P., Papanicolauo, A., and Denton, C. (2004). Neuroimaging in reading research. In N. Duke and M. Mallette's (eds.), *Literacy research methodologies* (pp. 252–86). New York: The Guilford Press.

Fox, M. (2001). *Reading magic.* San Diego, CA: Harcourt.

Farzee, Marla. (2006). Roller Coaster. Boston: Houghton Mifflin Harcourt.

Frazier, B., Gelman, S., and Wellman, H. (2009). Preschoolers' search for explanatory information within adult-child conversation. *Child Development, 80*(6), 15–92. Doi: 10.1111/j.1467-8624.2009.01356x.

Gallagher, J. J. and Ascher, M. J. (1963). A preliminary report on analyses of classroom interaction. *Merrill-Palmer Quarterly, 9*(1), 183–94.

References

Gambrell, L. B. (1983). The occurrence of think-time during reading comprehension. *Journal of Educational Research, 75*, 144–48.

Gambrell, L., Block, C. C., and Pressley, M. (2002). *Improving comprehension instruction: Rethinking research, theory, and classroom practice.* San Francisco: Jossey-Bass.

Grasesser, A. C., McMahen, C. L. and Johnson, B. (1994) Question asking and answering. In M. A. Gernsbacher (ed.), *Handbook of psycholinguistics* (pp. 517–38). San Diego, CA: Academic Press.

Guthrie, J. and Ozgungor, S. (2002). Instructional contexts for reading engagement. In. C. C. Block and M. Pressley (eds.), *Comprehension instruction: Research-based best practices* (pp. 275–88). New York: Guilford.

Harmin, M. and Toth, M. (2006). *Inspiring active learning: A complete handbook for today's teachers.* Washington, DC: Association for Supervision and Curriculum Development.

Harvey, S. and Goudvis, A. (2000). *Strategies that Work: Teaching Comprehension to enhance understanding.* Portland, Maine: Stenhouse.

Hynes-Berry, M. (2012). *Don't leave the story in the book: Using literature to Guide Inquiry in early childhood classrooms.* New York: Teachers College Press.

Jacobs, H. (1989). *Interdisciplinary curriculum: Design and implementation.* Washington, DC: Association for Supervision and Curriculum Development.

Janssen, T. (2002). Instruction in self-questioning as a literary reading strategy: An exploration of empirical research. *Educational studies in language and literature, 2*, 95–120. http://dx.doi.org/10.1023/A:1020855401075.

Jones, J. and S. Leahy, (2006). Developing strategic readers. *Science and Children. 44*(3), 30–34.

Katz, L. (2010). Knowledge, understanding, and the disposition to seek both. *Exchange, 32*(6), 46–47.

Kelley, M. and Clausen-Grace, N. (2008). From picture walk to text feature walk: Guiding students to strategically preview informational text. *Journal of Content Area Reading, 7*(1), 5–30.

Kelly, M., Moore, D., and Tuck, B. (1994). Reciprocal teaching in a regular primary school classroom. *Journal of Educational Research, 88*(1), 53–62.

Kettmann-Klingner, J. and Vaughn, S. (1996). Reciprocal teaching of reading comprehension strategies for students with learning disabilities who use English as a second language. *The Elementary School Journal, 96*(3), 275–93.

Leven, T. and Long, R. (1981). *Effective instruction.* Washington, DC: Association for Supervision and Curriculum Development.

Lewin, L. (2010). Teaching critical reading with questioning strategies. *Educational Leadership, 67*(6). (online). Retrieved from http://www.ascd.org/publications/educationalleadership/mar10/vol67/num06/Teaching-Critical-Reading-with-QuestioningStrategies.aspx.

Lindfors, J. (1999). *Children's inquiry: Using language to make sense of the world.* New York: Teachers College Press.

Manzo, A. (1969), "Improving Reading Comprehension through Reciprocal Questioning." Unpublished Dissertations. Syracuse University.

McTigue, J., Seif, E., and Wiggins, G. (2004). You can teach for meaning. *Phi Delta Kappan, 62*(1), 26–31.

Mesmer, H. A. and Hutchins, E. J. (2002). Using QARs with charts and graphs. *The Reading Teacher, 56*(1), 21–27.

Myers, P. (2005). The Princess Storyteller, Clara Clarifier, Quincy Questioner, and the Wizard: Reciprocal Teaching adapted for kindergarten students. *The Reading Teacher, 59*(4) 314–24.

National Reading Panel. (2000). *Teaching children to read: An evidence-based assessment of the scientific research literature on reading and its implication for reading instruction.* Washington, DC: National Institute of Child Health and Human Development.

Ness, M. (2014). Helping elementary teachers to think aloud. *Reading Horizons, 53*(2). http://scholarworks.wmich.edu/reading_horizons/vol53/iss2/2.

Nolte, R. Y. and Singer, H. (1985). Active comprehension: Teaching a process of reading comprehension and its effects on reading achievement. *The Reading Teacher, 39,* 24–31.

Oczkus, L. D. (2010). *Reciprocal teaching strategies at work: Powerful strategies and lessons for improving reading comprehension* (2nd ed.). Newark, Delaware: International Reading Association.

Ogle, D. M. (1986). K-W-L: A teaching model that develops active reading of expository text. *The Reading Teacher, 39,* 564–70.

Palincsar, A. and Brown, A. L. (1984). Reciprocal teaching of comprehension fostering and comprehension monitoring. *Cognition and Instruction, 1*(2), 117–75.

Palinscar, A. M. and Brown, A. L. (1986). Interactive teaching to promote independent learning from text. *The Reading Teacher, 39*(8), 771–77.

Pearson, P. D. and Gallagher, M. (1983). The instruction of reading comprehension. *Contemporary Educational Psychology, 8*(3), 317–44.

Pearson, P. D. and Johnson, D. D. (1978). *Teaching reading comprehension.* New York: Holt, Rinehart, and Winston.

Peregoy, S. F. and Boyle, O. F. (2009). *Reading, writing, and learning in ESL.* Boston: Pearson.

Pilonieta, P. and Medina, A. (2009). Reciprocal teaching for the primary grades: "We can do it too!" *The Reading Teacher, 63*(2), 120–29.

Postman, N. and Weingarten, C. (1971). *Teaching as a subversive activity.* New York: Dell Publishing.

Raphael, T. E. (1984). Teaching learners about sources of information for answering comprehension questions. *Journal of Reading, 27,* 303–11.

Raphael, T. and Au, K. (2005). QAR: Enhancing comprehension and test taking across grades and content areas. *The Reading Teacher, 59*(3), 206–21.

Raphael, T. E and McKinney, J. (1983). An examination of 5th and 8th grade children's question answering behavior: An instructional study in metacognition. *Journal of Reading Behavior, 15,* 67–86.

Raphael, T. E. and Pearson, P. D. (1985). Increasing students' awareness of sources of information for answering questions. *American Educational Research Journal, 22,* 217–36.

Raphael, T. E. and Wonnacott, C. A. (1985). Heightening fourth-grade students' sensitivity to sources of information for answering comprehension questions. *Reading Research Quarterly, 20*, 282–96.

Rosenshine, B. and Meister, C. (1994). Reciprocal teaching: A review of the research. *Review of Educational Research, 64*(4), 479–530. doi: 10.3102/00346543064004479.

Ross, W. (1860). Methods of instruction. Barnard's *American Journal of Education*, 9, 367–79.

Ross, J. A., Hogaboam-Gray, A., and McDougall, B. (2003). A survey measuring implementation of mathematics education reform by elementary teachers. *Journal of Research in Mathematics Education, 34*(4), 344–63.

Rothstein, D. and Santana, L. (2010). Sharing the power of the question. *ASCD Express: What Does a Whole Child Approach to Education Look Like, 7*(13), 8–11.

Rothstein, D and Santana, L. (2012). Sharing the power of the question. *ASCD Express: What Does a Whole Child Approach to Education Look Like, 7*(13).

Rothstein, D. and Santana, L. (2014). The right questions. *Educational Leadership, 72*(2), 38–43.

Scardamalia, M. and Bereiter, C. (1992). Text-based and knowledge based questioning by children. *Cognition and instruction, 9*(3), 177–99.

Schuman, H. and Presser, S. (1979). The open and closed question. A*merican Sociological Review, 44*(5), 692–712. doi:10.2307/2094521.

Singer, H. and Donlan, D. (1989). *Reading and learning from text*. Hillsdale, NJ: Erlbaum.

Singh, M. (2014). What's going on inside the brain of a curious child? National Public Radio. http://blogs.kqed.org/mindshift/2014/10/whats-going-on-inside-the-brain-of-a-curious-child/.

Smith, F. (1994). *Understanding reading* (5th ed.). Hillsdale, NJ: Erlbaum.

Snow, C. (2002). *Reading for understanding: Toward a R&D program in reading comprehension*. Washington, DC: RAND Reading Study Group. Retrieved from http://www.rand.org/pubs/monograph_reports/MR1465/MR1464/pdf.

Society for Research in Child Development. (November 13, 2009). When preschoolers ask questions, they want explanations. *Science Daily*. Retrieved July 29, 2014 from http:www.sciencedaily.com/releases/2009/11/09111308254.

Sporer, N., Brunstein, J. C., and Kieschke, U. (2008). Improving students' reading comprehension skills: Effects of strategy instruction and reciprocal teaching. *Learning and Instruction, 19*, 272–86. doi:10.1016/j.learninstruc.2008.05.003.

Stahl, K. (2004). Proof, practice, and promise: Comprehension strategy instruction in the primary grades. *The Reading Teacher, 57*(7), 298–609.

Strauss, V. (2015). Retrieved from https://www.washingtonpost.com/blogs/answer-sheet/wp/2015/06/05/why-a-simple-30-year-old-chart-is-an-ingenious-teaching-tool-today.

Strickin, K. (2011). Hands-on reciprocal reaching: A comprehension technique. *The Reading Teacher, 64*(8), 620–25.

Taboada, A. and Guthrie, J. T. (2006). Contributions of student questioning and prior knowledge to construction of knowledge from reading information text. *Journal of Literacy Research, 38*(1), 1–35. doi: 10.1207/s15548430jlr3801_1.

Taylor, B. M., Pearson, P. D., Clark, K. and Walpole, S. (2000). Effective schools and accomplished teachers: lessons about primary grade reading instruction in low income schools. *The Elementary School Journal, 101*(2), 121–65.

Taylor, B. M, Pearson, P. D., Peterson, D. P, and Rodriguez, M. C. (2003). Reading growth in high-poverty classrooms: The influence of teacher practices that encourage cognitive engagement in literacy learning. *The Elementary School Journal, 104*, 40–69.

Therrien, W. J. and Hughes, C. (2008). Comparison of repeated reading and question generation on students' reading fluency and comprehension. *Learning Disabilities: A Contemporary Journal, 6*(1), 1–16.

Travers, R. (1998). What is a good guiding question? *Educational Leadership, 65*(6), 70–73.

Tyler, R. (1949). *Basic principles of curriculum and instruction.* Chicago: The University of Chicago Press.

van den Broek, P. and Kremer, K. (2000). The mind in action: What it means to comprehend during reading. In B. M. Taylor, M. F. Graves, and P. van den Broek (eds.), *Reading for meaning: Fostering comprehension in the middle grades* (pp. 1–31). Newark, Delaware: International Reading Association.

Wallace, V. and Husid, W. N. (2011). *Collaborating for inquiry-based learning: School librarians and teachers partner for student achievement.* Santa Barbara, California: Libraries United.

Weglinsky, H. (2004). Facts or critical thinking skills. *Phi Delta Kappan, 62*(1), 32–25.

Weiderhold, C. (1991). *The question matrix: Cooperative learning & critical thinking.* Resources for Teachers.

Westera, J. and Moore, D. (1995). Reciprocal teaching of reading comprehension in a New Zealand high school. *Psychology in the schools, 32*(3), 225–32.

Wiggins, G. J. and McTighe, J. (2005). *Understanding by Design, expanded 2nd edition.* Alexandria, VA: ASCD.

Wilen, W. (1991). *Questioning skills for teachers* (3rd ed.). Washington, DC: National Education Association.

Wilhelm, J. (2007). *Engaging readers and writers with inquiry.* New York: Scholastic Press.

Williams, J. (2010). Taking on the role of questioner: Revisiting reciprocal teaching. *The Reading Teacher, 64*(4), 278–81.

Willingham, D. (2015). *Raising kids who read: What parents and teachers can do.* San Francisco, California: Jossey-Bass.

Wood, K. (1984). Probable Passages: A writing strategy. *The Reading Teacher, 37,* 496–99.

Wurm, J. (2005). Working in the Reggio way: A beginner's guide for American teachers. New York: RedLeaf Press.

Yopp, R. H. and Dreher, M. J. (1994). Effects of active comprehension instruction on attitudes and motivation in reading. *Reading Horizons, 34*(4), 288–302.

Yopp, H. and Yopp, R. (2006). *Literature-based reading activities.* Boston: Pearson Allyn and Bacon.

Yopp, H. K. and Yopp, R. H. (2013), *Literature-Based Reading Activities: Engaging Students with Literary and Informational Text* (6th ed.). Boston: Pearsons.

LITERATURE CITED

Allard, H. (1977). *Miss Nelson is missing*. Boston: Houghton Mifflin.
Branzei, S. (2002). *Grossology*. New York: Price Stern Sloan.
dePaolo, T. (1975). *Strega Nona*. New York: Little Simon.
Hills, T. (2010). *How Rocket learned to read*. New York: Swartz & Wade Books.
McCarthy, M. (2007). *City hawk: The story of pale male*. New York: Simon & Schuster.
Meyer, M. (1987). *There's an alligator under my bed*. New York: Dial Press.
Moss, M. (2004). *Mighty Jackie: The strike-out queen*. New York: Simon & Schuster.
Raven, M. (2008). *Night boat to freedom*. New York: Square Fish.
Richardson, J. and Parnell, P. (2005). *And Tango makes three*. New York: Simon & Schuster Books for Young Readers.
Rohmann, E. (2007). *My friend Rabbit*. New York: Square Fish.
Swartz, S. (2009). *Butterflies of the sea*. New York: Dominie Press.
Van Dusen, C. (2009). *The circus ship*. Boston: Candlewick Press.
Willems, M. (2004). *Knuffle Bunny: A cautionary tale*. New York: Hyperion.
Willems, M. (2007). *Knuffle Bunny too: A case of mistaken identity*. New York: Hyperion.
Willems, M. (2010). *Knuffle Bunny free: An unexpected diversion*. New York: Hyperion.

About the Author

Molly Ness is an associate professor at Fordham University's Graduate School of Education. She graduated Phi Beta Kappa from Johns Hopkins University, and earned her PhD in Reading Education from the University of Virginia. Her research focuses on reading comprehension instruction, the instructional decisions and beliefs of preservice and inservice teachers, and the assessment and diagnosis of struggling readers. A former Teach For America corps member, she is an experienced classroom teacher. She is the author of *Lessons to Learn: Voices from the Front Lines of Teach For America* (Routledge Falmer, 2004). Her research has been published in national and international peer-reviewed journals including *The Reading Teacher, Educational Leadership, Reading Horizons, Journal of Reading Education, Reading Psychology,* and *Journal of Research in Childhood Education.*